CHILAR

CHILAR

Journey of a Lifetime

Kaye Kvam

©2016 by Kaye Kvam

All rights reserved: No portion of this book may be reproduced, stored in a retrieval system, or transmitted in any form or by any means, except for brief quotations, without the prior written permission of the publisher:

Published by Serving One Lord Resources, Sewickley, PA

ISBN 978-0-9823-1378-7

DEDICATION

For my son, Madison and my husband, Tom Mosley

Contents

Foreword	ix
Thank you	xi
Prologue	xiii
1. Opportunity Knocks	1
2. Considerations	4
3. A Courageous Decision	7
4. Summer Jobs	10
5. Doctor Zimmerman	13
6. Trip to Mexico	18
7. To San Ignacio	24
8. To Ajoya	31
9. The Ajoya Clinic	34
10. Our First Day	39
11. Mule Ride to Chilar	44

12. Dirty Pigs	50
13. Home Sweet Home	54
14. My First Day in Chilar	60
15. Montezuma Takes Revenge	65
16. Meal Time and Bath Time	71
17. Jack-O-Lantern	76
18. Dia de los Muertos	82
19. Consultas	88
20. A New Home	93
21. Thanksgiving	98
22. A Big Step Forward	104
23. Crecencio Pena	107
24. Caballo de Arriba	112
25. Pulling Teeth	116
26. Christmas and New Years	119
27. A Visit Back Home	124
28. My Birthday Celebration	128
29. Ernesto's Godparents	131
30. Unusual Labor and Deliveries	134
31. Jeronima	138
32. Adios, Chilar	142
Afterword	147

Foreword

Fifty years ago, a new girl showed up in the seventh grade at Vallecito Junior High School in Terra Linda, CA. From the moment I met her, I loved her. Funny beyond belief, with a face that contorted into some of the most hilarious expressions, Kaye Kvam has enriched my life ever since.

    We were best buds in high school. We roomed together in college. We had wonderful adventures traveling abroad. We stood beside each other as maid of honor in our respective weddings. We shared the trials and tribulations of motherhood and careers. Throughout it all, she has been a stalwart and steady presence in my life. I have always depended on her wise counsel and her ability to see the positive in any situation, no matter how dire it seemed.

    This book, *Chilar: Journey of a Lifetime*, focuses on just a year or so in the mid 1970s when an idealistic and irrepressible Kaye journeyed to Sinaloa, Mexico to try and make her mark on the world. I took her to the airport when she left, and I was there to hear all the incredible stories when she returned. This experience indelibly changed her and influenced the entire course of her life.

It has been my honor and privilege to be Kaye's scribe in the telling of this tale. As her ALS progressed, writing became more and more difficult for her, and the final chapters were written through unremitting pain and constant discomfort. But Kaye has faced adversity head-on her entire life, and this situation was no exception. No one could ever be stronger or more determined than this dear friend of mine.

This book is Kaye's legacy -- a gift to those she loves and a treasure for all those who have loved her.

Nancy Crawford Wise

July 2016

Thank You

I will always be grateful to the wonderful trusting villagers of Chilar who in 1974 took a young American woman into their home. Without knowing me at all, they generously fed me and gave me a place to live. They loved me as if I were one of them.

Six months later, I left far richer than when I arrived. I had learned that people are the same, no matter where they live, no matter their language or culture. I had trusted that things would turn out all right, even when I was pretty frightened. I came to love these people with all my heart.

I have two very dear people I need to thank. If it weren't for Sherree Funk, I would never have started or completed this book. In July 2015, I told her I was thinking about writing a book on my experience in Chilar, something I had been considering for years. She said, "Let's do it and I will help." She is an author so this was music to my ears. Because of her enthusiasm and encouragement, I started writing. She helped with editing as well. Thank you, Sherree for making a dream come true!

And then there is my dear friend, Nancy Wise. Nancy was my fingers. I wrote down my thoughts by hand and dictated them to Nancy, who quickly transcribed them on paper. Nancy, if it weren't for your typing and editing talents I would still be typing up Chapter One. You put in hours of your own personal time getting this all down on paper.

These two wonderful women I thank from the bottom of my heart.

Kaye

Prologue

October 5, 1974

"I've been in Mexico for just five days and already it feels like a lifetime. In just five simple days so much has happened. I've had many incredible experiences and now it's early morning and I'm waiting for a mule (and Ray) to take me to a place I have never been. A place that will be my home for six months . . . to a small mountainous village called Chilar. The future ahead looks so hard and so unattainable. I pray to God that I will be able to handle the challenges. I don't know, I just don't know..."

You might ask yourself how a naive young college student, from middle class America, found herself waiting for a mule in the mountains of western Mexico. Well, grab yourself a glass of wine, settle into that comfortable chair, and come along with me as I tell you the story of a journey that changed my life forever.

Chapter 1
Opportunity Knocks

One February morning in 1974, in the coffeehouse at the University of California - Davis, I had a conversation that would change my life. I'll never forget that day.

I parked my bike in the rack and dashed in to grab a quick bite. With only thirty minutes before my next class, I ordered a bagel with cream cheese and a small coffee.

"Kaye?" I heard as I paid for my purchase.

I turned and saw my friend Stacy waving at me to come sit with her. When I joined her, she showed me the Doonesbury cartoon in the *Cal Aggie*, the daily university newspaper. We both had a good laugh.

"Wish I could stay and chat, but I've got to get to class."

"Which one?"

"Anatomy and physiology, ugh."

"My next class is embryology, but not until eleven." Ignoring my comment about my rushed schedule, Stacy launched into a detailed description of a volunteer medical program she had visited over winter break, called Project Piaxtla. "David Werner runs it. He used to be a high school biology teacher from an alternative school here in California. He set up these clinics in the Sierra Madre Mountains of Mexico."

I glanced at my watch, but Stacy seemed oblivious to my subtle hint. She kept talking.

"Werner originally went into those mountains to study biology and to find an exciting field trip location for his students. When he got there, he was appalled by the lack of medical care he saw in the poor villages. He contacted some people he knew at Stanford University and asked for donations of medical supplies. Then he went back with a group of people who were willing to help, including his students. After a few more trips, he started his first clinic in Ajoya in 1966." Stacy smiled and took a breath. "That's where I went over winter break, Kaye. It was amazing." She went on. "Anyway, Werner became passionate about this work and quit his job as a high school teacher. He now has several clinics in the area."

Stacy's enthusiasm piqued my interest. I sat back in my chair, more interested in hearing details about this project than in getting to class on time. "How did you find out about all this?"

"My father told me about it. He's a doctor at Stanford."

I had a deep desire to help people in need of medical care. This seemed like a perfect opportunity to do just that. And to see if medicine was what I really wanted to do with my life. "Does this guy only take high schoolers on his trips?"

"He's willing to take college students who are interested in medicine. But he prefers they make a commitment of at least four to six months."

The more Stacy talked about Project Piaxtla, the more fascinated I became. It sounded like an exotic adventure that was right up my alley. But could I afford to take six months off from school?

Stacy suddenly realized the time. "Oh! I'm so sorry. You said you had a class to get to, and I probably made you late."

"That's OK. I'm glad you told me about this."

As I rode my bike to class, I thought about Project Piaxtla. I was a starry-eyed 21-year-old hoping to make a difference in the world. I had dreamed of someday joining the Peace Corps. Or maybe working on the ship called Project Hope. Now I had another option. I wondered if working with Project Piaxtla could actually become a reality for me.

Chapter 2

Considerations

For as long as I can remember, I have wanted to help the sick. When I was in third grade, I found a baby bird in the woods that had fallen from its nest. It made me feel so good to nurse it back to health and watch it fly away. I tried the same thing with a baby squirrel, but despite my best efforts, it died. I cried as I placed its soft, tiny body in a size-five Keds shoe box and gave it a proper burial in the woods behind my house, near where I'd found it.

In that same year, my left knee suddenly became red, warm, and swollen. Doctors kept me in the hospital for days, performing lab tests, X-rays and invasive procedures. While I waited for a diagnosis, they put my leg in a cast, confined me to a wheelchair, and prescribed aspirin for the pain. After several weeks I was diagnosed with juvenile rheumatoid arthritis.

As I lay in the hospital with doctors analyzing my swollen knee, my mother was in the same hospital, being treated for breast cancer. My father repeatedly told me, "Mommy is getting better." But whenever I saw her, I knew she was dying. I remember thinking, as only a child can, how much I wanted to help Mommy and make her better. Unfortunately, this was not to be. My mother died shortly after I was discharged.

In high school I considered becoming a nun. I had a deep-seated faith and had always felt God placed me on this earth for a purpose: to help those in need. *The Flying Nun* was a popular TV show then. If I could have been a superhero nun like Sally Field, I might have signed on. But I envisioned real nuns living cloistered away, so I wouldn't be able to offer as much practical help for the poor as I wanted to. A career in nursing seemed like a much better option.

By the middle of March Stacy had an announcement to make. "Kaye, I've decided to go to Mexico and work for Project Piaxtla! I'm leaving September thirtieth. Do you want to join me?"

My mind raced with excitement. Me go with her to Mexico? Could I really take a year off school and go? My father wouldn't understand what a wonderful opportunity this was for me. But I knew he would let me go if I really wanted to, as long as I promised to return and finish my college education.

I wondered about the language barrier. Could I learn enough Spanish over the summer to communicate effectively? I had taken four years of French in high school. Weren't the two languages pretty similar? No worries. I would get a Spanish book and start studying right away. I had until the end of September.

And what about financial considerations? Could I afford it? I had some money saved, but it wasn't enough. I could work during the summer … as many jobs as necessary to make this work. After all, I had until the end of September, and school got out in May.

Then there was that "tiny" issue of my lack of medical

knowledge. Could I gain some medical experience before I left? Could I learn enough? I'd figure out something. After all, I had until the end of September.

The end of September arrived with startling speed.

Chapter 3
A Courageous Decision

Nancy and me

When I told Stacy I would go to Mexico with her, I thought of it as an adventure and a dream come true. Little did I know what was truly in store. If I had known the harsh realities of life in Chilar or the challenge and danger of the Mexican mountain villages, I might have responded differently. Thank goodness I was young, stupid, and idealistic because that one decision changed my life in ways I could never have imagined.

Before spring quarter ended, Stacy and I met several times to discuss our trip to Mexico. At one of those meetings Stacy introduced me to a budding new medical profession she was considering. It was called Physician Assistant.

"PAs are medically trained providers who, after graduating from a two-year program, function much like physicians. They treat patients who present with common medical conditions."

"The training must be pretty intense," I said.

"It is. But Stanford has a program, and I think it'd be great for you." She rifled through her pack and handed me a brochure.

I had considered going to medical school. But I was afraid that the tremendous debt I'd incur and the many years of training might cause me to give up my goal of working in medically underserved areas. I'd probably have to get a high-paying job in a large city hospital in order to pay off my financial obligations. At the time, I planned on applying to nursing schools for the following year.

I tucked the brochure into my backpack, promising myself I'd look into the PA program later.

My top priority was finding a cheap place to live for the summer. Nancy, my best friend from seventh grade, and roommate at Davis, offered to share an apartment with me. We rode our bikes to the campus housing office in ninety-eight-degree heat, arriving hot and sweaty. The air-conditioned office was a welcome relief.

As we pored over the bulletin boards, Nancy found an incredible deal: a two-bedroom furnished apartment, with swimming pool for $200 for the entire summer. Our plan to wait until the last week of school to get the best deal had paid off. Subletters were desperate to lease out their apartments for the summer for whatever price they could get.

We called the number right then and there, asked a few

questions, and decided to take it, sight unseen. When we visited the apartment later that day, it was perfect. It was small and cozy, but we each had our own bedroom. And that swimming pool sealed the deal. Once final exams were finished, we spent an afternoon and evening packing up Nancy's car with boxes and moving into our new home.

The next step was finding jobs. Nancy landed a waitress position at The Nut Tree, a restaurant in nearby Vacaville, working four hours a day, five days a week. She made great money from tips at the popular eating spot. I took a job in a convalescent hospital as a nurse's aide. The pay wasn't great, so I supplemented my income by cleaning apartments in the evenings and on my days off.

Even though I was working two jobs, Nancy made more money than I did and she had more free time. I remember coming home exhausted to find her counting her tip money on the kitchen table. It was nice that she often brought home free food from the restaurant, which she generously shared with me. However, while I bathed, dressed, and fed elderly patients at the convalescent hospital, she spent her mornings lounging by the pool.

Oh, why hadn't I applied for a job at The Nut Tree?

Chapter 4
Summer Jobs

As it turned out, my work at the convalescent hospital proved very valuable. I learned much about caring for the elderly, but I also discovered a great deal about myself. I was able to find the courage and inner strength to do work that wasn't very pleasant, in a place that shocked and at times frightened me.

Before that summer I had never been exposed to anyone suffering from dementia. I'd never seen a body lying in bed twisted and rigid from stroke. I had never bathed adults or changed their diapers. I'd never worked in a place where the smell of urine was everywhere, despite the staff's best efforts to keep things clean.

Initially, it was hard for me to see elderly patients in wheelchairs lining the hallways. Some smiled and greeted me as I passed by, while others just stared into space, expressionless. Occasionally I heard a patient cry out from a room. At first I couldn't understand why no one ran to see what was wrong. After a while I understood this was a daily occurrence for that patient. The experienced staff knew when the yelling was real and when it was just the dementia speaking.

One day I was assigned to work in the wing that housed the elderly patients with severe dementia. As I stood at the nurse's station, waiting for my assignment, a female patient came up to me and yelled, "I'm the devil and I can kill." I nearly bolted. But just then, one of the seasoned nurses approached her, took her arm, and said calmly, "Now, Betty, why don't we go back to your room and listen to some music?"

That nurse's calm example taught me how to react to terrifying situations without taking them personally. She taught me how to take charge and defuse difficult situations in a gentle yet firm manner. Such lessons continue to serve me well today.

In that same wing was an elderly male who would sneak out to the parking lot to pick up cigarette butts. He'd put them in his mouth and chew, even though he had no teeth. He then went back to his room and spit them into a pile by the side of his bed. No sooner did we clean up his pile than he'd be out foraging again for more cigarette butts.

Then there was George. We had to keep a close eye on him, because he had a habit of wandering into females' rooms and climbing into bed with them. I soon learned those were the screams we had to pay attention to!

The work was exhausting and overwhelming, and every day I witnessed many bizarre behaviors. Even so, I believed I was making a small difference in the lives of the patients I cared for, just by being kind and respectful in my interactions with them.

One of my patients, Virginia, had a rare neurological condition, which caused her to lose coordination and speech. She was confined to a wheelchair and flailed about uncontrollably whenever she tried to move. Since I'd never seen anyone with this weird, debilitating disease, taking care of Virginia initially scared me. My job was to feed Virginia. This had to be done slowly and with much care as she had lost her ability to chew and swallow in a coordinated fashion. Her sudden body jerks and flailing made this particularly difficult.

Over time, as I came to know the woman inside the body, her outside appearance fell away. Virginia communicated with me through her eyes. After a while I could tell when she was frustrated or content, and I figured out what she liked and disliked. As the days passed, we established a comfortable, trusting relationship and I grew quite fond of her.

One day, when I came into work, I learned she had died. Apparently, one of the nurse's aides hadn't been careful enough when feeding her, and Virginia aspirated and died.

Death was a frequent visitor at the convalescent hospital, but none affected me as deeply as Virginia's.

Most days, after my shift at the convalescent hospital, I rode my bike to my second job, cleaning apartments on J Street. I loved riding in the cool of the evening, hearing crickets chirping and smelling Mother Earth's sweet aroma of honeysuckle and clover. These bike rides were healing for me as the tension and pent-up emotion of the day's work faded away.

Cleaning apartments also helped me decompress. It was mindless work, but seeing the results of my scrubbing, mopping, and vacuuming was satisfying. Cleaning gave me a sense of control that I didn't always feel with my job at the convalescent hospital.

Chapter 5

Doctor Zimmerman

As the summer progressed, I wondered how I might get more medical experience than what the nursing home offered. I didn't want to be completely clueless when I went to Mexico that fall.

While cleaning an apartment one night, the solution came to me. UC Davis had a medical school. Why not go to their office, explain my plans, and ask if I could train under a physician? Surely I wasn't the first person to request this type of help.

The woman at the administrative office was very nice and listened with interest. "I know exactly the doctor who will do this." She wrote a name on the back of her business card and handed it to me. "Dr. Zimmerman is a family physician at the UC Davis Sacramento Medical Center. He teaches in the family practice residency program there. I'm sure he'd be interested in helping you."

I called the number the next day and spoke with Dr. Zimmerman's nurse. She told me he was busy seeing patients, but she would talk with him and call me back.

To my surprise, she returned my call the very next morning. She told me he would be delighted to help train me. "He'd like to start with two afternoons a week." That sounded perfect to me.

I changed my schedule at the convalescent hospital and started my training the following week.

When I told Stacy about my great opportunity, she was excited for me. She'd been training with a few doctors her father knew at the Stanford Medical Center and was finding the experience invaluable.

She recommended I get a book she had purchased called *Donde No Hay Doctor* (Where There Is No Doctor), written and illustrated by David Werner. "This is the medical manual used by the villagers and volunteers in the Project Piaxtla clinics. It explains how to diagnose and treat many of the health concerns found in the rural mountains of Sinaloa."

I ordered the English version. I also bought *Spanish Made Easy*.

As I was leaving the apartment for my first day with Dr. Zimmerman, Nancy came out in her swimsuit and sunglasses, towel and baby oil in hand. "Good luck with your training," she said as she headed to the pool to work on her tan.

I held back my bitterly jealous reply.

But as I gazed out the window of the bus to the medical center, both excitement and trepidation filled me. I was excited that someone was willing to help my dream become a reality. But I worried that the training might not be adequate or relevant for my work in Mexico. I only had six weeks more weeks of summer. I should have allowed more time for this.

At least my forty-minute bus trip to and from Sacramento would give me some good time for studying Spanish.

The bus dropped me off three blocks from the medical center. I walked up to the building, took a deep breath to work up my courage, and ventured in. The Family Practice Clinic was on the first floor. Taking another deep breath, I opened the door and walked up to the smiling receptionist.

"Can I help you?" she asked.

I told her who I was and that I was there to shadow Dr. Zimmerman.

"Oh, yes. He's expecting you. Have a seat. His nurse, Penny, will be right out."

I sat beside a young mother holding her fussy baby. As I looked around, I noticed people of all ages and many ethnicities, a majority of them Hispanic.

Within a couple of minutes, Penny came out and called me.

"It's been a very busy day for us," she said with a welcoming smile as she led me down a short hallway. "Dr. Zimmerman is an excellent physician and teacher. You'll learn a lot from him."

The stocky woman's friendliness and kind words relieved my anxiety. Penny waved me into a small office. "He'll be with you as soon as he's finished with his current patient."

In no time at all, Dr. Zimmerman walked in wearing a white coat, a stethoscope, and a broad smile. He immediately put me at ease. I could tell from his eyes that he was a kind man. "You must be Kaye." He shook my hand, introduced himself, and grabbed a chart. "Come on, let's go see some patients together."

All day long, he had me listen to hearts and lungs, feel bellies, and look into ears and mouths with him. One of our patients turned out to be the fussy baby I'd sat next to. Through a translator, we learned that he'd had a fever off and on, was not eating normally, and had been tugging on his right ear. Using the otoscope, Dr. Zimmerman showed me what an ear infection looked like.

Between patients, we talked about Project Piaxtla and what I would be doing in Mexico. He showed me his copy of Lange's *Current Medical Diagnosis and Treatment*, saying he thought I might find it helpful. One glance at the table of contents, and I jotted down the title so I could order it for myself.

Dr. Zimmerman was also familiar with David Werner's book, *Where There Is No Doctor*. "The UC Davis medical school has it listed as a required text for their students on rural rotations."

I left the office exhausted but exhilarated. Wow! I had hit the jackpot. This was exactly the type of hands-on training I needed to prepare me for Project Piaxtla.

As my training progressed, I got to observe Dr. Zimmerman do several procedures, including removing splinters and suturing lacerations. I also had the opportunity, after watching him do several female exams, to perform a pap smear on a willing patient under his supervision. He even arranged for me to follow the orthopedic technician, and I learned how to cast a broken arm by practicing on the technician!

Dr. Zimmerman readily took me under his wing and he was a wonderful teacher. I will forever be grateful for his kindness and generosity.

Near the end of September, Stacy and I began planning the last-minute details of our trip. We figured we could save money by taking a midnight flight from San Francisco to Los Angeles. I asked my friend Tim if he could pick us up at the airport and drop us off at the bus station. It would take several different bus rides and a train to get to Ajoya where the main clinic was.

Little did I know that, in fact, Ajoya would not be my final destination. Getting there would require a mule ride even further into the mountains.

We made our reservations and I started packing my bags, excited about the adventures ahead.

Chapter 6

Trip to Mexico

September thirtieth finally arrived. Because our flight was at midnight, I hugged my parents goodbye at home. My friend Nancy drove me to the airport and waited with me at the gate.

I had decided to apply to nursing school, but the applications would arrive while I was gone.

"I'm not sure what the mail situation will be in Mexico. You can open anything that looks important," I reminded Nancy. "I'll be back in January to complete the applications and send them in."

We were deep in discussion when Stacy arrived with her parents. We introduced ourselves and stood around making awkward small talk. Soon the boarding announcement was made over the loudspeaker.

Nancy - my dear, loving, and practical best friend - turned to me and said, "Kaye, I can't believe you are really doing this and that they are actually letting you!" We hugged each other tightly. She was worried for me. But I was excited for what my future might hold. I waited for Stacy as she hugged her parents. Her mother cried as her father stood by quietly. In a way, I was glad my parents weren't there. We grabbed our book bags and walked down the jetway together, waving back at the three of them until we could no longer see their worried faces.

I could tell Stacy was as excited as I was. We were on our way to becoming healthcare volunteers in Mexico. We had to pinch ourselves to make sure this was really happening. We talked nonstop and arrived at LAX in no time. Even at 1:15 in the morning we weren't the least bit tired. When we got off the plane, my friend Tim was at the gate to greet us. "Thanks, Tim. This is so kind of you. I know you have an early class."

I had met Tim my sophomore year when we lived in the same dorm at UC Davis and became friends. He was now in his first year at the University of Southern California pharmacy school.

I introduced him to Stacy on our way to the baggage claim area. "We have two huge backpacks and my guitar." Tim wasn't surprised. For any college student in the 60s and 70s who played guitar, this was a necessary piece of luggage. Frankly, I couldn't bear the thought of not bringing it. Playing guitar and singing songs by my favorite artists, like Peter, Paul & Mary, James Taylor, and Carole King gave me great joy.

We crammed everything into Tim's blue Volkswagen bug and off we went. Our bus didn't leave until 3:40 a.m., so we had a little bit of time to kill. Tim drove us around Los Angeles, showing us the USC campus, his pharmacy school, and where he lived. None of us minded that it was the middle of the night. We went down the brightly lit Sunset Strip before he dropped us at the Greyhound bus station.

The bus station was surprisingly busy for such an early hour. We bought tickets to Calexico, California and boarded the bus. We had the worst possible seats - non-reclining and directly across from the smelly bathroom. To make it even worse, a baby nearby screamed off and on for most of the trip. Sleeping was out of the question.

The hot and stuffy bus was completely filled with Spanish-speaking passengers. I wondered if they would be crossing the border with us once we arrived. It proved to be a "local" bus, which stopped at every small town along the route. At least we could get off and buy food and drink along the way. But instead of the normal three to four hours, it took us six to reach our destination.

Exhausted, we arrived at Calexico, where we grabbed our bags, and along with our fellow passengers, simply walked into Mexicali. The border crossing certainly would not be so easy today. As soon as we crossed the border, kids wanting to sell us all kinds of trinkets, candy, and gum bombarded us. Taxi drivers shouted to attract our attention. We needed transportation to get to the train station. Stacy, whose Spanish was better than mine, found us a taxi driver who would take us there for just one American dollar.

We couldn't buy our train tickets until we had our backpacks inspected by customs officers. I'm sure we looked like every other college student in the mid-1970s traveling the world. We met some other college kids while waiting in line. Two college girls from California were on their way to Mazatlan to study Spanish. A young man was traveling around the US and Mexico. The customs officer went through all of our bags. He noticed our medical books and the box of medicine Stacy was bringing to the clinic. In broken English, he asked our purpose for travel to Mexico. "We will be volunteering in a clinic in western Mexico for six months," we answered confidently.

"You need visas," he said, pointing to a long line across the room.

We hadn't counted on this, but after getting through customs, we exchanged money and proceeded to get our visas. Then we bought some food and drink for the train ride. Finally done with everything, we couldn't wait to get on the train.

We had purchased first class tickets because they were surprisingly cheap and we hoped to finally get some sleep in our own quiet compartment. The eighteen-and-a-half-hour trip would be much more pleasant that way. Unfortunately, due to jerky stops and train whistles, we were only able to sleep in short intervals.

When I couldn't sleep, I studied Spanish. Stacy had informed me that David Werner might not let me stay if I didn't speak any Spanish. This had me worried. I would be devastated if I traveled this great distance only to be told to go home until I learned the language. I found that possibility terrifying.

Whenever I left our compartment to go to the bathroom or stretch my legs, I was shocked by the difficult traveling conditions for everyone not in first class. Mexican families with small children were crammed into noisy and crowded cars with all their belongings. I felt guilty every time I went back to the quiet compartment we had all to ourselves.

I was also shocked by the poverty I saw from the train window. There were slums surrounding many of the cities we passed through. Shacks in the middle of nowhere had garbage strewn all around. Buzzards picked at animal carcasses that lay by the side of the tracks.

It was a far cry from the view out my train window the previous summer. I had traveled to Europe where charming small towns, beautiful cathedrals, and well-manicured countryside gave a different impression. I couldn't understand why the Mexican government didn't try to improve the living standards of their people. Why were so many living in such poverty? Did Mexico have no middle class?

When we arrived in Culiacan at six o'clock the next morning, it was already ninety degrees and horribly humid. This was the rainy season, so it poured heavily off and on during the day. We were so hot and sweaty that we went straight to the nearest bathroom to change into lighter clothing. It wasn't long before we were hot and sweaty again.

> October 2, 1974:
> "I think I'm experiencing culture shock because everything and everyone is grossing me out. For one thing, the lack of sanitation is unbelievable. The people really don't care how smelly and dirty the bathrooms are, no matter how nicely dressed they are. The toilets are broken; they don't flush, and of course there are flies over everything."

At least we could wash our hands in cold running water. We were glad we brought our own soap and toilet paper. I just wondered how long that roll would last us.

The other thing that disturbed me was how the Mexican men would stare, as if they were mentally disrobing us. It made us very uncomfortable. It was as if they had never seen an American girl before. Maybe they hadn't. I was grateful that they didn't whistle and call after us like the Italian men I encountered the previous year in Europe.

The next phase of our travel would be a bus ride to San Ignacio and from there, another bus to Ajoya. With any luck, we would arrive at the clinic that night. Luckily, the bus station was next door to the train station. Under the leering gaze of the Mexican men, we lugged our baggage to the bus station where we were greeted with even more staring.

The only bus to San Ignacio would leave in six hours. After purchasing tickets, we looked around the bus station and realized that the cafe was back at the train station. Once again, we dragged our bags back to the train station under the watchful eyes of every Mexican man there. I felt totally naked by the time I ordered my chicken enchilada and Coke.

After lunch, back at the bus station, Stacy took two plastic chairs, stretched out on them, and promptly fell asleep. How could she sleep with all these men staring at us? Tired as I was, I couldn't nod off. By this time, the bus station was busy, and now everyone was looking at us. As the only Americans, we stuck out like sore thumbs with our backpacks, book bags, and my guitar. I opened *Spanish Made Easy* and focused on my studies.

Chapter 7
To San Ignacio

The bus finally arrived after what seemed like an eternity. It looked like a beat-up old school bus with wooden boxes and crates of vegetables tied to the roof. Inside, the seats were well worn and uncomfortable; the open overhead bins were crammed with luggage and bags of merchandise.

As we took seats several rows back, I noticed a clay figurine of Mother Mary on the dashboard along with rosary beads and crosses hanging from the mirror. Above the driver's head was a cross with Jesus hanging on it and below that, a picture of St. Christopher and one of Pope Paul VI. I laughed to myself when I saw this and thought: with all this protection, nothing's gonna stop this bus from getting to San

Ignacio.

The bus driver, a handsome man with a mustache, muscular arms, and a rather large belly stepped in. He somehow squeezed behind the steering wheel and manually closed the door. He turned the key and after several loud, unnatural cranking noises, the engine started. It then took several clutch-grinding attempts to get the bus into first gear. We lurched forward. Every time he went to shift there was more grinding. This didn't sound good to me, but he seemed to take no notice, and off we went.

Torrential rain had been coming down all day. I noticed that the windshield wipers didn't work very well, and vision out the front window was limited. I found this a little alarming, but once again the bus driver seemed unconcerned. Somehow he was able to see well enough to maneuver onto the chaotic main boulevard. Driving was random and fast even in heavy traffic. Our driver managed to dodge cars coming from all directions. At this point, it became very clear to me why so many religious icons were needed.

Once we made it safely through the city of Culiacan, we drove along miles of narrow roads filled with potholes. We sped around every blind curve we encountered - on the wrong side of the road. The bus had no air conditioning and was hot and humid. Frankly, I couldn't tell if I was sweating from the heat or the terrifying drive.

We'd been on the road for nearly two hours when the bus came to an abrupt stop. The driver donned his rain poncho and got off. Through the wet windshield, I could see him talking with some men pointing toward a rapid, swollen river. On closer examination, I saw remnants of a low-lying bridge. Great, I thought. The bridge is washed out. I could see the city of San Ignacio across the flooded river, but it looked impossible to get there.

"Why in the world didn't they tell us about this when we bought our tickets?" I looked at Stacy in exasperation.

"Perhaps they didn't know. Or maybe they knew the bus would make it one way or another, either today or tomorrow." Stacy laughed.

I can't stress enough how Stacy kept me going. If not for her, I would have turned back miles earlier. Since she had been to Ajoya, she knew what to expect and seemed to take everything in stride. Thank goodness she was there to talk me down from that 'cliff' of culture shock I'd been experiencing regularly since we crossed the border.

As Stacy and I continued to watch, wondering what was going to happen next, we noticed a large primitive wooden raft on pontoons come into view. It had three cars on it. It docked on a makeshift ramp and the cars drove off. It looked like we were next to be ferried across. Fortunately the rain stopped temporarily. Everyone got off the bus while the driver carefully drove it onto the raft. Then we all walked onboard, and stood close to the bus, holding on for dear life. A flimsy rope banister was the only thing separating us from the swift river.

The raft was attached to some kind of a pulley system consisting of a large, thick rope secured on either side of the river. Evidently this rope not only guided and pulled the raft but also prevented it from being washed downstream. On either side of the raft, several men with large, long poles pushed us as well until we arrived safely on the other side.

The resourcefulness, ingenuity, and determination of these men really impressed me. I'm sure for them this was nothing out of the ordinary. For me it was nothing short of a miracle. "This would never happen in the United States," I said. Stacy agreed.

Although I wasn't Catholic, I crossed myself several times as I re-boarded the bus and uttered a silent prayer of thanksgiving to the Holy Virgin Mother Mary.

In no time at all, we arrived in San Ignacio only to discover that we had missed the *routa* or bus to Ajoya. We met Antoine, the owner of the *routa,* who Stacy knew from her visit last year. "You're going to have to wait until tomorrow," he told us. "That *routa* usually runs daily, but the schedule sometimes depends on weather conditions or other emergencies."

I was excited that I could actually understand a little of what Antoine was saying in Spanish, but disappointed in what I'd heard. I turned to Stacy and was about to ask her what we were going to do next when Antoine invited us to stay with him and his family. How generous of him, I thought. I was so glad he and Stacy were friends. We took him up on his offer. *"Si! Muchas gracias!"*

That evening, Antoine's wife prepared a wonderful meal for us. Afterwards I played guitar and we sang to their five adorable children. I couldn't believe how hospitable Antoine and his family were. I couldn't help but wonder how many American families would have opened their homes and fed strangers under the same circumstances.

We went to our room early that night, thoroughly exhausted. "Antoine is considered rich around here," Stacy explained, "because he's one of the few people in town with a shower and a toilet." To our dismay, the toilet didn't flush so we had to use the outhouse. Nevertheless, we were excited to finally have beds to sleep in. We were less excited about the cockroaches scurrying around our room. I found it interesting that these disgusting insects didn't discriminate against rich families or poor families, but made themselves at home everywhere. Everyone seemed to accept them as a part of life.

We put our pajamas on, rolled out our sleeping bags, and climbed on top of them. I was almost asleep when I felt something crawl across my face.

> October 3, 1974:
> "It didn't gross me out that there were cockroaches and bugs all over the place. The part that bothered me the most was at night when they crawled all over our beds and us."

Early the next morning we woke suddenly to a high-pitched squealing sound. We both sat up and looked at each other. "They must be slaughtering a pig," Stacy surmised.

I couldn't believe it. They were actually killing a pig right outside our room. As it turned out, they didn't just kill one pig that morning, but several.

By the time we got dressed, packed our things and walked over to the main house, we noticed vultures circling overhead where the men were butchering the pigs. A couple of hungry birds, eager for their turn at the carcasses, hopped nearby. I was in shock. I had never seen any animal butchered before. My only other experience remotely like this was watching my dad clean a fish he had just caught before my mom cooked it for dinner. Thankfully, fish didn't squeal.

After breakfast, which to our relief did not include ham or bacon, we thanked Antoine's wife profusely for the delicious meal and for her hospitality. With her permission, we stored our bags there and took off in search of mules to take us to Ajoya.

The village of San Ignacio was clean and quaint, much to my pleasant surprise. Cobblestone streets surrounded the central town square. We walked by small open storefronts along plain dirt roads and saw tiny cafes attached to homes. Women, whose young children wandered around everywhere, ran these family businesses. The older children were in school. The stores were packed with everything one could need: flashlights, batteries, detergent, canned goods, coffee, Wonder Bread, and snacks.

The day was hot and humid with no rain to cool us off. We knew we couldn't drink the water, so we drank what seemed like a hundred Cokes that day. Each store had refrigeration, and the cold Cokes were so refreshing. We also bought ice cream and cookies, and Stacy introduced me to delicious "Carlos Quintos" chocolate bars. From then on, I kept an eye out for those chocolates in every little town.

During our search for mules, we met many friendly and helpful people but after exhausting all our leads, we came up empty-handed. It looked like our only hope of getting to Ajoya was going to be the *routa*. We would have to wait and see if the *routa* would be returning later that day.

    While eating a late lunch at one of the family-run cafes, we heard that the bus was back in town. We finished quickly and hurried back to Antoine's house. Sure enough, it had returned and was leaving for Ajoya at five o'clock.

Chapter 8

To Ajoya

The *Routa* to Ajoya

We grabbed our bags, got our tickets, and thanked Antoine and his wife once again. Rounding the corner we caught our first glimpse of the *routa* and I nearly died on the spot. Even Stacy was surprised. "The bus I took last year was a lot better than this one."

This bus was no more than a beat-up open flatbed truck with the cab doors removed. In the flatbed, chairs and benches were nailed down for seating. The truck was loaded with live chickens in a cage, bags of merchandise and clothing, a couple of blankets, and some suitcases. A spare tire was tied down with rope. We added our backpacks and guitar to the mix. As I walked by the cab, I noticed rosary beads on the mirror, a familiar picture of the Virgin Mary, and a cross with Jesus on it. I knew we were in good hands.

Stacy and I jumped on and joined three other passengers in the back. The bus jolted forward. It looked like this was going to be another bumpy ride. We held on tight to our seats.

> October 3, 1974:
> "The trip on the *routa* was simply unbelievable. Rarely was there even a road to follow. We went across streams, along riverbeds, and through wilderness that was so untamed I didn't think we had any chance of getting there."

Halfway to Ajoya, when we thought it couldn't get any worse, we got a flat tire. In almost total darkness, with only the light from one flashlight, the men tried to change the tire.

Pointing to my guitar, the driver looked at me and said, "Musica?" He wanted me to play while they worked. What a sight that must have been! Stacy and I sang American folk songs under a bright, starry night while the crickets and frogs sang along. "Puff the Magic Dragon" never sounded so good.

After awhile, the men weren't looking too happy. Apparently, they didn't have the right tools and they couldn't get the tire off the rim. "Another *routa* will be coming. That one might take you to Ajoya." It didn't sound like a sure thing, however. They continued working on the tire and I continued my playing.

Within a half hour, another bus did come by from Ajoya heading towards San Ignacio. This bus looked very similar to the one we were on. It however was almost empty, except for a few boxes. It occurred to me two "routas" traveled in opposite directions every day when possible. That way, one could assist the other if problems arose. Not a bad plan, I thought.

With some difficulty, they were able to turn the newly arrived bus around. Once this was accomplished, they transferred our belongings onto it, and then we climbed on. As we were pulling away, Stacy overheard the driver tell the two men left behind that he would return that night with the correct tools needed to change the tire.

With nothing but headlights to direct us through the pitch black, I was sure we were blazing our own trail. Stacy, of course, took it all in stride. I found when my heart wasn't in my throat, it was pounding loudly in my chest. At several points along the perilous route, I thought the bus might topple over and I would need to jump off to safety.

It was nine-thirty that night, October 3rd, when we finally arrived at Ajoya. Stacy was yawning and looked tired. I was more than tired; I was physically and emotionally drained. I had noticed during our trip to Mexico that the discomfort from my arthritis was more noticeable. This was probably because of the humidity and the physical strain of carrying a heavy backpack. But I had never let chronic pain from my arthritis bother me or hold me back. I wasn't about to let it bother me now. I tried to ignore the pain so most people didn't even notice my condition.

Chapter 9
The Ajoya Clinic

Mike and Kerry at the Ajoya clinic

Ray and Martin from Project Piaxtla greeted us as we stepped down from the *routa*. They grabbed our bags and led us by flashlight through the dark, unpaved streets to the clinic. It was eerily quiet. The evening's warmth and dampness created a variety of unfamiliar sweet aromas. Except for an occasional dog barking, the silence was deafening. I wondered if everyone in Ajoya had already gone to bed.

They led us to a whitewashed adobe house. I noticed the sign,

Clinica, above the entrance. When they opened the door, we saw, lit up by several kerosene lamps, a circle of healthcare volunteers in what must have been the patient waiting room. They were discussing their patients and the medical problems of the week.

David Werner came over to welcome us. He was a slender man, of short stature, with thinning brown hair, a bushy beard, and thick eyebrows. His weathered face made him look older than his forty-one years. I noticed he had an odd limp. When he shook my hand, I could see the muscles in his hands were atrophied and his fingers had limited movement. His thumbs didn't move much at all.

Stacy had told me that David had some kind of neuromuscular disorder and had numerous surgeries on his hands to make them more functional. I couldn't believe it when she said he had even assisted on some of his own hand surgeries. He reminded me of a rugged outdoorsman who did not let his disability hold him back. A lesser man would have returned to the states and gone back to teaching high school. Instead, he got on mules and traveled into the mountains to set up clinics in remote areas and even wrote and illustrated his own medical book. I could relate to his tenacity and I admired him for it.

"Come, join the circle." David motioned for us to take a seat. Introductions began. A Quaker couple, Mike and Kerry, were high school teachers from Colorado. Lyn was an emergency room nurse from San Francisco, and Michael a general surgeon from Stanford. Then there was Ray, a pre-med student from the Boston area. Last to be introduced was Martin, born and raised in Ajoya. He was David's protégé and second in charge. Apparently, years ago David recognized Martin as a smart eighteen-year-old with an interest in medicine. The young man was well respected in the community, an important factor. David realized that anyone he chose to train from the community had better be well liked; otherwise, people simply would not come to the clinic for medical care. Fortunately, they trusted Martin, so David taught him some basic medicine as well as English. He even brought Martin to California a couple of times for more medical training.

When I looked around the room, I was so impressed with everyone. Mike and Kerry had already been working at the clinic for a month. Lyn and Michael had arrived two days before, and Ray was a veteran of six months, although most of his time was at another clinic further in the mountains.

The meeting ended soon after the introductions. Stacy and I decided to sleep out on the covered porch that was attached to the clinic. Stacy fell asleep immediately. I swear that woman could fall asleep anywhere.

As I was about to drift off, I heard a loud buzzing sound. It got louder and louder the closer it got. It was low flying, whatever it was. Suddenly, with a thud, it hit the wall behind me and fell to the ground right next to my head. Not knowing what it could be, I bolted out of my sleeping bag and grabbed Stacy's flashlight. There, squirming on its back, was a huge black, hard shelled beetle. I later found out the name of this ugly, but harmless beetle: *bombilla*. I took my shoe and brushed it off the porch. Not long afterwards, I heard a pig scurry up and start eating it, crunching away and oinking with delight. I was too exhausted to be grossed out. I rolled over and fell into a deep sleep.

The roosters woke us up early the next morning. We rolled up our sleeping bags, got dressed, and put our things away. Stacy grabbed her box of donated medicines to take to the kitchen, which had been turned into the clinic's pharmacy. When we walked in, we jumped back when we saw the frogs, hundreds of them, covering the floor. We had to be careful not to step on them. Apparently last night's rain had driven them in, but before long they hopped back outside and were gone. That was an interesting experience so early in the morning, I thought.

The kitchen, I mean pharmacy, had tons of shelves packed with all kinds of medicines, including penicillin and amoxicillin. As David requested, Stacy left her box on the table so he could go through it later. He would inventory what she brought and file the medicines on the appropriate shelves.

We needed to bathe, but breakfast took first priority. We walked uptown for breakfast with the family Stacy stayed with last year. Stacy's family was incredibly warm and friendly and prepared us a wonderful meal of handmade corn tortillas, eggs and refried beans.

October 4, 1974:
"It is so organic here. Everywhere one looks there are pigs, chickens and dogs walking about freely and no one seems to care. This morning we were eating breakfast and a pig walked in to eat too, rummaging about our feet. Before we even sat down, our host had to shoo a chicken off the chair. Chickens seem very fond of sitting on chairs here."

After breakfast, we went down to the river to bathe. With a half-slip and a tee shirt on, I washed up as well as I could. We even washed our hair. The water was icy cold but it felt so good to finally be clean.

We ate with a couple of different families Stacy knew that day, and each meal was so delicious. For lunch we had corn tortillas with refried beans and cheese, and for dinner corn tortillas with more refried beans, soup, and fresh squash. Corn tortillas and refried beans were staples of their diet. "We can drink the water here," Stacy said, "It's safe." It was refreshingly good.

"Are those your only shoes?" Stacy pointed to my beat up tennis shoes. "Let's get you a pair of sandals."

On our way back to the clinic, we stopped by a small, family-run store where I bought a pair of *huaraches*. I also purchased some postage stamps and some *Carlos Quintos* chocolate bars. Stacy knew the owners, so we spent time visiting with them. Stacy seemed to know everyone in this small town. I thought it odd she had made so many friends in the short time she had visited last year. It occurred to me that this probably had a lot to do with the culture here. These people readily opened their arms to strangers with tremendous hospitality and friendship. I found this a refreshing change from the culture in which I was raised.

Chapter 10

Our First Day

David Werner's Book

Our first day in Ajoya proved beyond all doubt the great need for these medical clinics.

Early in the morning several men arrived carrying a woman on a makeshift stretcher of burlap wrapped around two strong tree limbs. Ten days prior, she had stepped on a nail and had developed a bad infection. Her foot had become gangrenous. The men from her small village had carried her down mountain passes, through rough terrain and across several rivers to get to the clinic - a distance of about thirty miles. There were enough men traveling so they could trade off carrying her, without needing to stop for long.

This was so unbelievable to me. These people had to endure hardships and overcome obstacles that seemed overwhelming. For them, it was simply the lifestyle they were accustomed to. In my short six-month stay, I would witness this kind of human courage and determination time and time again.

David cleared the table. "Put her up here. Careful now." Michael and Lyn gathered up the equipment they would need. The woman was in obvious pain. Stacy and I watched, fascinated, as Michael numbed the area with lidocaine, and then with a sterile surgical blade started cutting off dead tissue from the sole of her foot. In places he had to cut right down to the tendons. When he realized the foot was beyond the care he could provide in the clinic, he stopped. He wrapped it up and Lyn injected the patient with a huge dose of penicillin.

Michael turned to Martin. "She really needs to get to the hospital as soon as possible. She will definitely need intravenous antibiotics, and most of her foot might need to be amputated." Martin was able to arrange for a truck owner in Ajoya to take her all the way to Culiacan. They left that very morning.

No sooner had this woman left than another emergency came in. A twelve-year-old boy had been kicked in the face by a mule. He had a huge bloody laceration on his right cheek. All the rooms in the clinic were busy so Michael took care of the young boy on the porch where Stacy and I had slept. We watched as he injected lidocaine into the wound, cleaned it thoroughly, and then skillfully closed it. What once had been a large gaping hole was now a neat, three-inch suture line.

Both of these cases were amazing for us medical newbies to watch and it was even more amazing that we didn't get sick while watching!

Martin looked at Stacy and me. "Do you two think you could give this woman a bath?" he asked, indicating the clinic's only inpatient, an elderly woman with heart failure. We did the best we could under the circumstances. We heated water and used a bar of Ivory soap and some clean rags for a sort of sponge bath. It was not quite how I did it in the Davis convalescent hospital, but good enough.

After lunch, and as part of our training that day, Stacy and I, along with local healthcare aides, practiced giving each other injections and drawing each other's blood. It was fun until the person drawing my blood had to stick me three times before successfully locating a vein. Ouch.

While Stacy followed Kerry around seeing patients with coughs, rashes, and other minor complaints, I got to observe the local seventeen-year-old dentist. I was surprised that he had his very own dental chair in one of the rooms at the clinic. He showed me how he pulled teeth, which I learned he'd been doing since the age of fourteen. He even did a few fillings. I couldn't wait to write my dad, the dentist, that night about my experience.

It was five o'clock and with no more patients to see, we closed the clinic.

I saw David and Ray talking to each other, occasionally glancing in my direction. I wondered what they were discussing. Had I performed OK that day? I sure hoped so.

Soon David walked over. "Ray will take you to another clinic tomorrow morning. Does that sound all right?"

"Sure, I'm ready," I blurted out.

"You'll be going by mule to Chilar. There's no road, no bus. Ray has already been there for six months. He can train you while you learn Spanish." He studied me doubtfully. "Maybe you can take over the Chilar clinic when Ray returns to the States."

I summoned my confidence and said, "I'm ready for the challenge." Ray smiled and turned away. I wasn't sure what he thought. In reality, Stacy and I were crushed, because we had hoped we would be working together in the same clinic during our time in Mexico. Stacy didn't yet know where she would be assigned. She might stay in Ajoya or be sent to another village in the mountains.

David had more to tell me. "You need a Spanish name. Kaye would just confuse the locals. It sounds like the Spanish word, *que,* which means 'What?'"

He suggested "Katalina." From that moment on I was known as Katalina. Stacy later told me she hoped my name would be *cochita,* which means little piglet. We had a good laugh over that one.

After dinner, Martin suggested we might be more comfortable sleeping in the clinic's loft. That sounded like a good idea, so we lugged all our stuff up there. But as we rolled out our sleeping bags, we noticed millions of cockroaches, so we opted for the covered porch again. It was raining, and we knew we would get a little mist on us from time to time, but that was better than having cockroaches crawling over us all night.

Before going to bed, I wrote this in a letter to my parents:

"I feel like Jane Goodall in deepest Africa. Right now it's dark outside and raining with thunder and lightning (but a warm rain) and I'm writing this by kerosene lamp. Stacy and I are feeling overwhelmed and bummed because this will be our last night together for who knows how long. Tomorrow I go by mule to Chilar. What am I doing? Will I ever learn Spanish? Will I be of any use in this remote clinic? At least David is letting me stay . . . Gulp!"

I took out my guitar, and sang a few songs with Stacy before going to bed. If I'd known what was in store for me the next day, I might not have slept so soundly. I thought the trip to Ajoya was frightening, but it was a piece of cake compared to the next day's trip to Chilar.

Chapter 11
Mule Ride to Chilar

The night before, I had asked Ray how and what I should pack for the mule ride. He was very vague about it and never really gave me a straight answer, so this city girl did the best she could. I got all my clothes, belongings and books neatly packed and ready to go.

Like clockwork, the roosters woke us up bright and early the next morning. Stacy and I went to yet another friend's house for breakfast. The Mexican coffee is incredibly delicious. It is brewed with freshly ground beans and for cream we used evaporated milk. That morning, I drank three large cups.

Returning to the clinic, I found my letter to my parents and handed it to Stacy. "Would you please mail this for me?"

"No problem. I have a few letters to mail too. They can go out on the *routa* later today."

I sat down to wait for Ray and started to reflect on the past several days in Mexico. How amazing, I thought. I took out my journal and started writing.

October 5, 1974:

"I have been in Mexico for just five days, and already it feels as if it's been a lifetime . . ."

It wasn't long before Ray arrived with the mules. He took one look at my pile of stuff and said curtly, "You have to repack. You're bringing way too much. You can only bring what will fit on the back of the mule. That guitar will definitely have to stay." I was frustrated that he hadn't told me this the night before. Now I had to go through everything again and lighten my backpack and book bag.

I left a small bag with a few clothes, my camera and film, and my two heavy medical textbooks. I kept the English version of *Where There Is No Doctor,* my *Spanish Made Easy* text, and my dictionary. I looked at Stacy. "Can you keep these for me?"

"Of course." I handed the small bag and my guitar over to Stacy. "I'll take good care of everything, especially your guitar."

I looked wistfully at my guitar case. "I should be back sometime in January on my way back to the States. I guess I can take everything home with me then."

Ray tied my red backpack and sleeping bag onto the back of the mule. I swung my book bag over the saddle horn. Ray noticed I needed a flashlight, so I quickly bought one at a nearby store, along with some extra batteries. That was everything. We were finally ready to go.

I turned to Stacy and hugged her. "I'll send word when I get settled in Chilar," I assured her. "And let me know as soon as you find out where you'll be working."

After several failed attempts to get on my huge mule, a villager suggested I stand on a nearby rock. He then walked the mule over to me. From my elevated perch I was able to put my foot in the stirrup and swing my other leg over my bags to the other side. It was pretty obvious to everyone this was my first time on a mule (or any four-legged beast of burden for that matter).

Ray tried to encourage me. "You'll be fine on this mule. I've got the more spirited one." Thank goodness for that, I thought, as I smiled tentatively. I didn't have a clue how to ride this thing and I didn't want any trouble.

I waved goodbye to Stacy and the others and we started off. Though the hard saddle was super uncomfortable and I felt quite a strain on my hips and knees, I thought it was kind of cool. I was actually on a mule. I was riding it into the mountains of Mexico to a remote village. What an exciting adventure that would be! "Wait 'till I write Nancy and my friends and family about this," I thought. "They won't believe it!"

October 6, 1974:

"I have never been so scared in my life and for such a long stretch – nine hours. (The trip usually took 4 to 5 hours.) My mouth was completely dry and I was almost in tears the entire time. I was so freaked out. Most of the time I kept my eyes closed and prayed. I just could NOT believe the trail we were taking, plus my butt and joints were killing me."

Instead of a gradual ascent up the mountains, we shot straight up and down them. We had to make numerous river crossings on our mules. Sometimes the water was swift and deep, reaching almost to the saddle. Thank God the mules were strong, surefooted, and able to swim, because more than once I was convinced we would be swept away.

I was afraid Ray didn't know where he was going. Several times we had to backtrack. No matter how often I asked him how much further we had to go, he never gave me a straight answer.

Occasionally we would stop at an isolated wooden shack at which Ray asked directions. This was a blessing to my aching body. The inhabitants usually offered us water, which I always drank from atop my mule. I was determined to not get off my mule until we reached Chilar.

Unfortunately I had to get off several times to relieve myself in the bushes. At one home we were invited in for a bite to eat. All I can say is it was hell trying to remount the mule, so I always looked for a high spot to stand on to make it as easy as possible.

At one point, Ray decided we needed to switch mules. I guess he felt we weren't making fast enough progress and thought this might help. Either that, or he wanted to get rid of me, and was hoping the more spirited mule would carry me swiftly into the sunset, never to be heard from again. I didn't really want to, but we made the switch anyway.

The minute I got on, "Super Mule" took off galloping. Terrified, I held on for dear life as we went crashing through the thick brush. Ray yelled after me. "Pull back on the reins as hard as you can." With a jerk and all the strength I could muster, I did, and Super Mule finally stopped, but not before the thorny branches ripped my collar off and tore several holes in my shirt.

That mule tried to throw me off a couple more times during the journey, but I held on. One time while we were stopped for directions yet again, I noticed a big tree nearby with a low-lying branch sticking out. Unfortunately, so did Super Mule. Slowly . . . ever so slowly, he inched his way over to this branch, and went under it. I don't know why I didn't pull back on the reins or pull the reins to the right or the left to avoid it.

Have you ever done the limbo under a branch, in a saddle, on top of a mule before? Well, neither had I, but somehow, to my amazement, I was able to stay on. Except for a small scratch on my nose, I emerged unscathed. Super Mule must have been amazed as well, because from that moment on he seemed to behave himself, at least until the end of the trip.

As we rode further into the mountains, the vegetation became thicker. There were more trees, with vines hanging down from them. It didn't seem as hot or humid as before. Eventually, we emerged onto a well-worn path, lined with banana and mango trees. Though I didn't know it, we were getting close to Chilar.

Soon, without warning, Super Mule took off, galloping as fast as he could. I pulled back on the reins but to no avail. All I could do was cling tightly, with both arms wrapped around his neck, hoping I wouldn't be thrown off.

We galloped into an area with a few wooden shacks. Pigs and chickens scurried out of the way. He raced into an open corral and stopped abruptly. We had arrived. Super Mule must have known we were close to Chilar, and that's why he took off so fast. I think he was as relieved as I was that the nightmare was over. After nine hours, he was ready for some food, and more than ready to get me off his back!

Ray rode up behind me and got off his mule. Slowly, more and more villagers came out to meet us. They exchanged greetings with Ray and then stared at me - men, women and children. I tried my best to smile and thought, "*Okay, now is my chance to make a good impression. I will just get off this mule as gracefully as possible . . .* " The next thing I knew, I was flat on my face, on the ground, on top of a cow patty. I looked up and everyone just stared. I struggled to get up, stiff and sore, brushed myself off, and smiled. "*Bonjour*." Ha! I was so incredibly exhausted that I couldn't even say hello in Spanish.

Yes, I had finally arrived at Chilar.

Chapter 12

Dirty Pigs

My Chilar Family

Under the watchful eyes of the villagers, Ray grabbed my belongings and took me to the home of Socorro and Crecencio, where we had dinner. "This is Katalina. She will be taking over the clinic after I leave. Could she stay with you for a while until I can find her a more permanent place to live?" They nodded.

Except for a word here or there, I couldn't follow their conversation. I remember thinking this family sure had a lot of kids.

It was pitch black by the time we finished dinner. They lit a couple of oil lamps. "I'll come back in the morning and take you to a place where you can bathe." Ray then left for the clinic where he slept.

Socorro, with all her children in tow, led me to a small cot and showed me where I could put my things. She asked "pee, pee"? I nodded yes. She said something to the kids who, with a flashlight, led me outside to the back of the house. For some reason, several pigs came along. I realized this outdoor area was considered the "women's bathroom." So I hid behind some bushes and relieved myself. I was glad I had some toilet paper with me.

I was surprised the kids didn't go behind bushes, but went to the bathroom right there in the open. Maybe because it was so dark and no one could see very well? But why did the pigs follow us? I could hear them grunting and eating something but had no idea . . . unless . . . No, it couldn't be... It was too dark to be sure.

The children led me back to the room, and watched as I got undressed. I rolled out my sleeping bag and climbed in. The kids had never seen a sleeping bag. It felt so good to be horizontal and off that mule. I fell fast asleep. During the night, one of the little girls climbed into bed with me. Needless to say, I didn't get much sleep after that.

I finally woke up about seven o'clock. The family had been up for nearly two hours. I got dressed, grabbed my dictionary, and found Socorro with Maria, her twenty-three-year-old daughter, and a few of the children in the kitchen. Crecencio, the father, was already working on his farm or *milpa* located high up on the side of the mountain.

Maria poured me a cup of coffee and helped Socorro make breakfast. I was grateful that they washed their hands before making the corn tortillas. We ate fresh tortillas and refried beans and I noticed that I was the only one that morning who got an egg with my meal. It was another example of how these people were so generous with what little they had.

The kitchen had a door, actually a small wooden gate, to the outside, which was rarely closed during the day. As we ate, dogs, pigs and chickens wandered freely in and out. Socorro and Maria would shoo them away, and most of the animals would stay outside. One pig, however, would always return, aggressively looking for food scraps under the table, pushing our legs aside. Even though Socorro and Maria would take a stick and swat it away, it would always sneak back in. Eventually, no one noticed its presence except for me. Stupid, obnoxious pig!

After breakfast, Maria and the kids took me to the bathroom. It almost seemed like a social event, with all the females going together. The pigs followed in hot pursuit. It didn't take long before my suspicions from the night before were confirmed. I found a bush to hide behind while everyone else lined up against the back wall of the house. I could see why the woman and girls wore dresses. It made going to the bathroom easier and provided some semblance of privacy.

One of the younger girls couldn't find a spot against the wall, so she was forced to squat in the open. I watched in horror as a pig waited with open mouth under her for that special treat. Was this the same pig from breakfast, I wondered? When the little girl wasn't going fast enough, the pig nudged her with its snout, causing her to fall over. She had just gotten back up again when the scene repeated itself. Wasn't anyone going to do something?! Somebody, please, throw a rock or hit this pig with a stick! This was gross! Make it stop! Instead, they laughed at what was happening. No one seemed bothered by it, including the little girl. Now I understood why everyone went to the bathroom against the wall. It was to prevent these sneak attacks. I was appalled. For me, this meant war. From that moment on, I never went to the bathroom without a stick or a handful of rocks in case the pigs tried anything with me, which they did, several times.

  Occasionally, my "evil twin" would make certain noises when she walked past the pigs on her way to the bathroom. This would excite them. She would then go behind a bush and make more sounds. They would move closer and closer, grunting happily, expecting a mouthful of gourmet treats. Just when they were about to pounce, she would swat or throw rocks at them and off they would go, squealing. They soon learned not to mess with me . . . I mean her, my evil twin.

  In a letter to my parents, I wrote this about the pigs: *"They are like garbage disposals and are always grunting and licking up something . . . Yuck!"*

  Previously, I thought pigs were adorable. But now, after my breakfast and bathroom experiences, I found them stubborn, dirty, and totally disgusting.

Chapter 13
Home Sweet Home

Chilar

October 15, 1974:

"Chilar is a very tiny village high in the mountains. It sits above a small river, tucked between two mountains. There are perhaps thirty homes (more like shacks) in town with no running water or electricity. All drinking water is carried up from the river. Only one street (dirt) runs through town, and it is usually covered with cows, mules, chickens, dogs, cats, pigs, and *muchachos* (kids). There are lots and lots of kids here, and they are all so beautiful."

After breakfast, Maria told me about her family, with assistance from my Spanish dictionary. Her parents, Socorro and Crecencio, had a total of ten children, ranging from three to twenty-three years of age. "Three of the older children live elsewhere: two in Mazatlan and one in Los Angeles." She smiled, trying to help me understand. The children living in Chilar, besides Maria, were twelve-year-old Guadalupe, also called Lupe; ten-year-old Leticia; Marisella, eight; Raymond, six; Verhenia, five; and baby Crecencio, age three.

Maria told me she had been married twice before. "These two are my children." Enrique, nine months old, was lying on her lap breastfeeding. Ilatio was five.

She explained slowly and in very simple Spanish how couples got married in Chilar. Basically a man would take the woman with him up into the mountains for several days. When they returned, they were considered man and wife. It was hardly a sacred ceremony. Though most people were Catholic, this was the accepted way, since there was no priest in Chilar most of the time. At least they didn't have to worry about messy divorces, I thought.

"Occasionally," Maria said, "a desperate, lonely man from another village further in the mountains comes to *robar* (kidnap) a woman, forcing her to go off with him to be his wife." Suddenly I understood why the women made a social event out of going to the bathroom. It made sense that they always traveled in groups, never straying far from town alone.

Maria grew angry remembering. "They were *cochinos*." She was referring to the two men that had "married her." "They left as soon as I got pregnant." She and her children were forced to move back in with her parents.

Maria was so wonderful, I thought. I couldn't imagine any man leaving her. I'm sure moving back home caused some concern for Crecencio and Socorro. It meant less room in the house, crowded sleeping arrangements, and more mouths to feed. But somehow they made it work. That's what families did in this culture.

The other thing that impressed me about this culture was the abundant love they showed their children. The babies and toddlers in particular were the center of everyone's attention. As the children grew older, their job, among others, was to look after the younger kids. In this family, five-year-old Verhenia looked after three-year-old Crecencio. She liked to pretend she was his mommy and followed him around constantly, trying to pick him up and hold him. He wanted nothing to do with it and would run from her, protesting. It was a continual game of cat-and-mouse between them.

Toddlers who weren't potty-trained ran around bare-bottomed all day with no diapers. Boys just wore just shirts, if anything, and the girls, little dresses. I'm sure this made life easier as it meant less laundry to wash and no diaper changing during the day. The toddlers just went freely outside whenever and wherever they wanted, and the pigs usually took care of clean-up. At night they wore diapers, however, to protect other family members sleeping on the same cot.

Socorro was definitely the disciplinarian in the family. I saw her get mad often. It seemed like she was always yelling at the kids for something. Although she was nice to me, I was actually a little afraid of her, as were the kids. She was strict, well-organized, and hardworking, and each morning assigned the children their daily chores. Those chores were age specific, and included such things as sweeping dirt floors, picking up clothes, washing laundry in the river, gathering wood for cooking, feeding the animals and bringing water up from the river. Socorro was the general in charge in this family. Her determination ensured there was food on the table, the kids were clean and dressed, and the family cooperated under tight living conditions.

Crecencio was quite different. He rarely got mad, and when he did, it was usually because of the animals underfoot. Like Socorro, he worked very hard. But he was generally quiet and sweet-tempered. Whenever I smiled at him, he smiled back and shyly looked away. The little kids ran and jumped into his lap when they were tired or needed safe refuge. Sometimes I found him helping the younger family members with their homework. Although his formal education was limited, he knew enough to help the little kids with simple math and reading.

I was a bit surprised that children in this remote village attended school. Education in Chilar was sporadic. When a teacher was available, he or she taught children of all ages in a one-room schoolhouse. This schoolhouse also doubled as the village meeting hall and church. It was also a gathering place for holiday celebrations like Christmas.

Evidently, the current teacher had been in Chilar since September, but was leaving in December. No one seemed to know if he or his replacement would return in the spring. Usually, someone would come for a while at least once a year. In spite of the inconsistency, the people valued the education for the children, convinced that it would prove helpful in their lives.

I got a better look at the house that morning in the daylight. I couldn't believe eleven people lived there, and now with me it was twelve. The house consisted of only three rooms: one totally enclosed interior room with adobe walls, and two partially enclosed exterior rooms, which included a kitchen and a bedroom. These partially enclosed rooms had two walls of solid adobe and two wood fences four to five feet tall, open to the outside.

Crecencio, with the help of some of the men in town, built this house. With nothing more than machetes and simple saws, they cut trees into supporting beams. Smaller tree limbs were tied together with rope and twine and fashioned into partial walls and fences. The tree limbs were also placed on top of the roof, supporting the handmade, kiln-fired clay shingles. Adobe bricks, also handmade, consisting of clay, sand, mud, and straw were used in the solid walls, which provided some protection from the wind and rain.

The interior room was where all the females and baby Enrique slept. There were two large cots and one small one. I slept in the small cot, with Verhenia as an occasional nighttime visitor. The rest shared the two larger cots. Crecencio Sr. slept with the boys, Raymond and Ilatio, on a cot in the partially enclosed bedroom.

I loved talking with Maria because I could understand her Spanish. She spoke clearly and always used simple words I could follow. While Maria and I talked, the kids hovered around me. They touched my hair, my face, my hands, my simple jewelry. They sat in my lap, put their arms around me, and sometimes, in an attempt to get my attention, put their faces directly in front of mine, blocking my view of Maria. It was great. I loved the way they were so comfortable with physical closeness and with touch. Being raised in a Norwegian family that never showed outward affection of any kind, I embraced this refreshing change wholeheartedly.

Maria and the children helped me a lot with learning Spanish. With the younger kids, I played a game of pointing to various objects and they identified them in Spanish. When I deliberately said the wrong word, they laughed. Such genuine laughs and beautiful smiles. So began my Spanish lessons. My relationship with the children  flourished with each passing day. I felt right at home, as if I was just another member of their very large family.

Chapter 14

My First Day in Chilar

"Katalina! Vamanos." Interrupting my Spanish lesson with Maria, Ilatio, the mayor of Chilar, and another man of obvious importance came to the house to take me on a tour. They wanted to show me the town and introduce me to the townspeople. I jumped up, eager to look around.

Our first stop was to meet a man who had lived five years in the United States. Ilatio thought we might enjoy conversing together, but it was almost impossible to understand his terrible English. In his broken English with some Spanish words thrown in, I was barely able to understand that a year earlier he had sustained a gunshot wound, which splintered his femur and cut a major artery in his thigh. Now he walked with a limp.

I noticed he carried a gun in a holster. I had noticed several other men with guns in holsters as we walked through town. I couldn't understand why they needed them. The town seemed peaceful to me and I saw no threat anywhere. *Did they just want to look tough? How dumb, I thought.*

As we left, waving *Adios*, Ilatio asked me, "Do you like *musica* and *bailando*?" (dancing.) I looked at him blankly. He grabbed my hand and we danced a little in the middle of the street. I laughed and said, *"Si!"* They took me to the home of an accordion player. He and a few other men were sitting around laughing, drinking beer, and getting drunk. I was unimpressed with this introduction and a bit disgusted. I had grown up in a family affected by alcoholism. My dad was an alcoholic, and I hated what it did to him and our family.

Despite my own misgivings, such behavior was totally accepted, and this musician was held in high regard. Apparently music, dancing, guns, and booze were a big thing in this town. Frankly, it turned me off. But out of politeness and fear (they *did* have guns), I smiled and shook their hands, saying *"Mucho gusto conocerlo"* (nice to meet you.) I couldn't wait to get out of there and was totally relieved when we did.

As we walked the entire length of town, I noticed two horse corrals and houses of various shapes and sizes. Some were wooden shacks like Crecencio's while others were constructed entirely of adobe. Some were well kept while others were more dilapidated. A few of the adobe structures were whitewashed, including a tiny store and the schoolhouse.

As we continued our walking tour of Chilar, families came out of their houses to have a look at me. Ilatio introduced me as the new *doctora* in town. When I smiled, they smiled back. That's when I noticed that many of the adults had terribly decayed and rotten teeth. Sugar cane was a favorite treat in the Sierra Madres, and years of chewing cane had left their mark. It was obvious that nobody practiced oral hygiene here. I thought of the seventeen-year-old dentist in Ajoya and what a field day he would have up here. I wondered if he could teach me how to pull teeth.

As it turned out, I returned to Ajoya in late November for some training and I *did* learn how to pull teeth. But at the time the thought of getting onto another mule sent me into a panic. The pain of my first mule ride was still fresh in my mind and I vowed never to get on a mule again! I would rather walk! Or ride a helicopter!

The children followed alongside us everywhere we went. I was astounded at the size of families here. Some of the children grabbed my hand and walked with me for a while. The bashful ones would come up, touch me, and then run away, smiling and laughing. Unlike the adults, they had beautiful white teeth.

At the schoolhouse, the teacher came out to greet us and showed me the school. Inside was a large room and, to my surprise, a cement floor. There were tables and chairs, some benches and shelves. The young man was very pleasant and his Spanish, like Maria's, was perfectly understandable. It was interesting to me how I understood the Spanish of some villagers better than others. This held true even when I became more proficient in Spanish. I figured it was due to regional accents, enunciation, or speed.

By the time we returned to Crecencio's house, Ray was waiting for me. "I want to take you to my favorite bathing place. It's called *del oso*. (the bear) Grab your stuff and let's go." It took us what seemed like an hour to hike there, but boy, was it worth it. It was like something you would see in a National Geographic magazine, secluded and beautiful. Huge white rocks, heavy vegetation, and greenery surrounded a small

pool filled by several tiny waterfalls. It felt like we were in a jungle. The water was so clean and refreshing.

Ray bathed downstream and I bathed in the pool. It felt so good to finally be able to take all my clothes off and thoroughly wash my body. Ray told me the water was clean enough to drink. I didn't drink it, but I did brush my teeth in the pool.

For lunch Ray had brought some tortillas filled with frijoles. We sat on top of one of the rocks, with the sun warming us, and ate. It was so heavenly to be eating fresh, homemade food in such a beautiful spot. We talked a little about our families and school, but mostly we just sat in silence, enjoying the sun and our surroundings. We gathered up our things and made the long hike back to town.

That night, Ray took me to Trinidad's house for dinner.

Trinidad's whitewashed adobe house was one of the nicer ones in Chilar. It was very well kept. I enjoyed the girls of this family during my months in Chilar. Margarita was fourteen and she had some younger sisters. They had an outdoor kiln where I could watch them bake bread from time to time.

I came to appreciate this family and their warm hospitality.

Margarita and I became good friends. Some days I'd go with the girls to wash clothes or to collect water. They were well practiced carrying the buckets on their heads. They found it amusing that I could only carry them by hand. Other days we just visited and laughed together. Extremely bright, Margarita helped me perfect my Spanish.

I was not only falling in love with my new surroundings but with the people as well.

Chapter 15
Montezuma Takes Revenge

The next morning after breakfast, Ray took me to the clinic. To get there we had to jump from rock to rock over a thirty-foot riverbed. Ray made it quickly across, and waited for me on the other side. I had to go slower because of my weak arthritic ankles. I almost made it, but near the other side I slipped and landed with both feet in ankle-deep water. Ray held back his laughter. He had no idea I had arthritis, and I wasn't about to tell him. I'm sure he assumed I lacked coordination.

We made our way up a steep, winding path to a clearing. The clinic, an adobe building with a large front porch, was the only structure there. We stepped inside to find sparse furnishings including a table, chair, and a small cot arranged on a clean dirt floor. One wall held shelves full of medicine bottles, supplies, and a few medical books. David's book, *Donde No Hay Doctor,* lay on the table with a stethoscope, blood pressure cuff, and flashlight. There was no running water or electricity.

We had only been there a few minutes when a mother arrived with her three-year-old daughter for a *consulta* (consultation.) She was concerned because her daughter had *granos*, discrete bumps on her arms and legs, some of which looked infected.

We examined her, and Ray surmised she had itchy bedbug bites and had been scratching them until some got infected. He handed the mother some antibiotic cream. "Apply this to the lesions twice a day. Wash the area before putting it on the bites."

Then he turned to me. "Could you show her how to do this?"

I put Band-Aids on some of the oozing, infected sores. I trimmed back the little girl's long fingernails. "If you keep them short, it will keep her from scratching," I told her mother. The girl was adorable.

After they left, Ray showed me some of the other creams and medicines he had on the shelves. There were medicines for different types of intestinal parasites, antibiotics for infections of all kinds, and some pain medications. There was even injectable iron and penicillin.

I took a deep breath. I obviously had a lot to learn. I was going to have to read up on these drugs to make sure I understood when to give them and at what dosage. I found an old, slightly outdated drug reference text in English. That would be helpful.

I soon realized that Ray acted like he knew a lot, but was not much of a teacher. He would spout lots of medical information when people were around, apparently to impress them. But when we were alone, he never gave a straight answer to my questions. It was frustrating.

Our next patient that morning was actually Trinidad, at whose house we had dined the night before. While getting on his mule that morning, he slipped and hit his genitalia on the saddle horn. Ouch. I stepped out of the clinic while Ray examined him. He sent him home with a painkiller and instructions to put frequent cold-water compresses on the area, and to wear some kind of support. Ray told him he would stop by his house to check on him in a day or two.

Francisco and his wife Josephina invited us to their home for lunch. On our way there, Ray told me about them. "Francisco and his wife are one of my favorite couples."

"Why's that?" I asked.

"Well, for one thing, they're super clean. They actually understand the concept of germs."

They had a small but tidy adobe house. Unlike the many

large families, they had only one son, Juan, six years old. I didn't know if this was their choice or if they couldn't conceive any more children.

When we arrived, Josephina provided soap and water to wash our hands before lunch. She served us delicious green bean soup with tortillas and pineapple. I noticed she was careful to keep the tortillas and pineapple covered to keep the flies and cockroaches off of them. This level of sanitation was a pleasant surprise. At Crecencio's house, nobody seemed to mind if the tortillas they were about to eat had recently been covered with cockroaches.

No animals were allowed inside Josephina's house. What a refreshing change that was. I could see why Ray enjoyed visiting and eating with them.

I asked Francisco where the delicious pineapple came from.

"It's from my orchard. Would you like to see it?"

"Absolutely!" We climbed a narrow path, quite high, to get to the orchard, tucked away in the middle of nowhere, in the jungle. Besides pineapples, he grew some oranges, mangoes, and bananas. It was beautiful and amazing.

How hard it must have been to clear out the jungle by hand with only a machete, burn off the undergrowth, dig up the ground with a hoe, and then plant these fruit-bearing trees. This was how the men of Chilar made their *milpas*, by slashing and burning the sides of mountains and planting their crops of corn, squash, or beans. We picked some ripe oranges. Ray returned to the clinic while I brought some of the oranges to Crecencio's family.

Maria and Lupe were on their way to the river with a huge pile of laundry. I asked if I could join them. They waited while I grabbed a few of my things. I watched as Maria and Lupe skillfully washed each piece of clothing using powdered detergent, pounding the clothing on riverbed rocks. It took a while, but I finally got the hang of it. We laid

the clothes out on a rock in the sun to dry. I doubted if I would ever get my clothes as clean as they did.

That evening, not feeling well, I skipped dinner and went straight to bed. I had gas and an upset stomach. Late that night, intestinal distress hit me full force. I ran outside just in time to vomit and have several bouts of diarrhea. I felt horrible. As I dragged myself back to bed, I heard what I assumed were the pigs going at it. I turned to look, and was shocked to see it was the dogs doing clean-up duty this time. Ugh! Such a sight made me nauseous all over again.

Throughout the night, I made several trips outdoors with nausea, vomiting, and diarrhea. Even feeling so sick, I couldn't help but notice how beautiful the sky was. The stars were so bright, clear, and gorgeous. Then reality set in and I would be sick again.

I was ill and in bed for three days. At one point I woke up to see Maria and Socorro looking down at me with worried faces. Dehydration from dysentery was a major problem in the Sierras, and sometimes caused death, especially in the younger population.

I heard Ray talking to my family. "Make sure she drinks this. It's *Suero para tomar* (rehydration drink)." The drink consisted of boiled water, some sugar, and a little bit of salt and bicarbonate.

On day two, although my diarrhea subsided, I had a fever and a horrible sore throat. Ray diagnosed me with tonsillitis and gave me penicillin. By the next day, I felt much better and was slowly getting my appetite back.

I think this episode was probably the sickest I have ever been in my entire life! Being sick in bed gave me plenty of time to start missing home, my family, and friends. A tremendous lightning and thunderstorm made me feel even more vulnerable and homesick.

From time to time, the villagers would also get Montezuma's Revenge, but not as badly as I did. I suspected it was due to contaminated water, particularly after a heavy rain.

Chilar sat on a small hill above the river. Water filtered into *posos* (holes) dug by the side of the river. The women used gourds to scoop water into buckets, which they carried on their heads back to their homes. They would then pour the water into big clay pots, where it was available for cooking and drinking. But when there was a heavy rain, all of the runoff from the outdoor bathrooms nearby would wash downhill and contaminate the *posos*. Even though we encouraged them to boil the water, many families didn't do this. I guess they had grown used to occasional bouts of diarrhea.

During the six months that I lived in Chilar, as careful as I tried to be, Montezuma's Revenge would visit me off and on. But it was never again as bad as this first time.

Chapter 16
Meal Time and Bath Time

Every morning before going off to the clinic, I helped my family in some way. Sometimes I helped grind the dried corn kernels into cornmeal. We used an old hand-cranked metal grinder. This was a lot harder than it looked, and after about ten minutes I was sweating and exhausted. Maria, on the other hand, could grind the kernels quickly and with ease.

Once the corn was ground we added water and salt to make a dough. Lupe, who did a lot of the cooking, with the help of Maria and Socorro, showed me how she rolled it into balls and patted it quickly back and forth with the palms of her hands, flattening it into tortillas. She then placed the tortillas on a searing hot metal sheet, suspended by rocks over a wood fire. With her bare hands, she turned the tortilla quickly, and somehow never burned herself. When I attempted to make the tortillas, they were misshapen, and lumpy. Invariably I would burn my fingertips trying to flip them over.

Maria would get a heavy cast iron frying pan and toss some pig's grease into it. From a large metal pot hanging by a hook from a ceiling beam (to prevent cockroaches from getting inside) she would spoon out pinto beans that had been soaking in water overnight and fry them. Nothing tasted better than these *frijoles* (refried beans) with fresh warm tortillas.

Some days I helped Maria, Socorro, and Lupe wash laundry in the river. Most of the time, however, I helped by bathing the children. Bathing for them was little more than playing and splashing in the river. They loved it when I scrubbed them down from head to toe using scented soap and shampoo. Sometimes, like the Pied Piper, I had a whole troop of kids from the village follow me to the river for a "bath."

Several kids were absolutely filthy with stringy, matted hair, wearing dirty clothes they'd been in for weeks. They usually came from the poorer families in town. I couldn't understand why personal hygiene wasn't that important to many of the villagers. Perhaps they just didn't know how the simple fact of washing hands could make a huge difference in the spread of certain diseases. Maybe if I could teach the children how important this was, things would eventually change.

While bathing the kids, I found all kinds of skin problems and infections. Little Crecencio had several oozing scabs on his head and it took a couple of weeks of scrubbing these areas and applying antibiotic ointment before they finally cleared.

The kids were always fascinated when I brushed my teeth in the river. Many had never seen a toothbrush or toothpaste before. I wondered how I might get toothbrushes and toothpaste for them to use. Maybe when I went back up to the States in January, I would be able to bring some back with me. (As it turned out, I was able to contact Colgate executives while home, and they donated a hundred toothbrushes and fifty small tubes of toothpaste. I gave them to the children and showed them how to use them.)

One time while bathing in the river, I noticed a funny odor drift by. I couldn't identify exactly what it was or where it was coming from and decided to investigate after I brushed my teeth. When I walked around a large rock and went upstream, to my horror I saw in the distance a large dead animal decomposing in the river. This was the water we had just bathed in and I had just brushed my teeth in it. Gross!

I walked back and gathered them up and out of that water. Bath time was over.

Most days after bath time, it was playtime. One bathing spot had a large rock and a pool at its base. The kids loved making a big splash jumping off that rock. It was so much fun to see them laugh and enjoy themselves. Even though they were poor and had hard lives, there was still plenty of time for hearty laughter, joy,

and fun. This made a big impression on me and the image of these children playing in the water has stayed with me my whole life.

There were days when I'd go by myself up to Del Oso to bathe. Maria had warned me and said it wasn't safe for me to go alone, but I ignored her advice. One time while bathing in the pool I noticed a snake slither through the water right beside me. You never saw anybody with arthritic joints move so fast from water onto land.

Another time I had just finished bathing and was getting dressed when several teenagers came traipsing down a path carrying a four-foot rattlesnake suspended on a pole. I wondered if they had been watching me bathe the whole time. As it turned out, they were on the main trail the men took to access their mountain fields, or *milpas*. All this time I had been bathing beside a busy trail and I didn't even know it. Needless to say, that was the last time I bathed there.

The rattlesnake was intended for dinner that night and the boys invited me to join them. I did and it was delicious. It tasted just like chicken, only with lots of tiny bones in it.

The only other unusual food I ate was not by choice. One evening Ray and I had been invited to dinner at one of the families' homes in town. Right away I noticed the wall next to the kitchen table was covered with scurrying cockroaches. I'd grown used to living with cockroaches, but this seemed a bit excessive. The mother prepared frijoles with tortillas for us.

We were both hungry. As we ate ravenously by kerosene lamp, I noticed several of the beans appeared darker than the others. I was almost finished with my meal when I moved the kerosene lamp closer to my plate, curious about those darker beans. That's when I noticed they had antennae and little tiny legs attached to them. My stomach flipped. Ray saw them too.

We stood up abruptly, thanked them for the wonderful meal, and left quickly. I felt a little nauseated and Ray thought the whole thing was funny. We never ate dinner with them again.

Chapter 17
Jack-O-Lantern

Victoria Bueno and her Store

October thirty-first was soon approaching. "Maria, have you ever heard of Halloween?" She had heard of it, but really didn't know what it was. "Well, on Halloween, all the children dress up in costumes and go door to door asking for candy." As I tried to explain this in my limited Spanish, she and some of the kids listening nearby smiled and laughed, fascinated at our odd custom.

"Here we celebrate *Dia de los Muertos* (Day of the Dead) around the same time," Maria said. "It's a religious holiday. We remember friends and family who have died." Maria told me about special food prepared for the day. "Someone butchers a pig for roasting. Women spend the whole day preparing tamales, chorizo, and blood pudding to share with everyone."

It was the first time I'd ever heard of blood pudding. To butcher a pig, they would bleed it completely after cutting a major artery from the neck. They caught the blood in a large pot, heated it over the fire, adding spices, onions, and fat, making a thick black pudding. Although considered a delicacy, I never had the courage to try it. I never had the courage to eat pig's feet or brains either.

Another part of the celebration of the Day of the Dead was a big dance party. People came to Chilar from all over the area for the festivities.

On my way to the clinic that day, my mind was racing. What if I showed them how we celebrated Halloween? The tiny store in town had candy and gum, paper, and bags. What if I drew funny pictures of kids dressed up in goofy Halloween outfits and put them in little bags along with the candy and gum? I could also make a pig outfit for Verhenia to wear. If I could get my hands on a pumpkin, I could carve that as well and put a candle in it for full effect at night.

"What do you think, Ray?"

He liked the idea. "Victoria might be able to help with the pumpkin. She owns that little store in town."

"I think I'll head down there and ask her."

"While you're there, do you think you could show Victoria how to change a dressing? Her neighbor, Jeronima, has a bandage she cannot change by herself."

"Sure, no problem." I grabbed the dressings and started off to

Victoria's house.

Victoria was different from the other villagers. She was extremely bright, intuitive, and seemed more worldly. I could confide with her about my feelings - how I missed my friends and family and wondered about my future. I even mentioned that I was beginning to feel like a drain on my family in Chilar. She really listened and seemed to understand what I was experiencing.

She lived with Miguel, a really nice guy who worshipped the ground she walked on. Victoria had two younger children, Celia, who was 6 years old, and Manuel, who was 8 years old. She also had a brother, Angel, who was 14. None of these children were Miguel's, although he treated them like his own. Celia and Manuel were brother and sister; Angel was their uncle.

I really enjoyed spending time with Victoria and in a short time we became friends. She even showed me how to make a dessert called "pancakes," flour tortillas made with brown sugar, cut up and placed in a brown sugar syrup. Delicious!

"Victoria, I have a plan for Halloween and I need your help. Do you know where I can get a pumpkin?" I tried to explain how I would carve it out for a Jack-O-Lantern. She thought she could get one.

"Great," I said. "I'll come back on the thirty-first and we can carve it together."

I bought some candy and other supplies from her store. I was so excited that this was all going to work out and asked Victoria to help me keep the secret.

She took me next door to see her neighbor, Jeronima. She was another really neat woman. She was always positive and laughing, and I could see why they were good friends. Jeronima had burned her arm in hot grease, but it was healing nicely. While changing the dressing, I noticed her left thumb was dislocated and stuck in an upright position. She had injured it a few years before. It didn't seem to bother her. I was amazed at all she was still able to do, including milking her own cows and taking care of her pigs and chickens.

I showed Victoria how to change the dressing. "You are Jeronima's doctor now." I smiled and left her some supplies.

Victoria seemed excited to learn something new. I had no doubt she was capable of doing a good job.

I left them, and returned to the clinic where I started preparing my Halloween surprise.

Ray was waiting for me when I arrived. "A man in the next town is pretty sick. I think he may have malaria. I'm going to travel there this afternoon and I'll be gone for a couple of days. Do you think you can handle the clinic on your own?"

I was nervous to be on my own at the clinic, but I said, "Sure."

Ray gave me instructions on some of the patients. "Consuela needs her daily penicillin shots." He was treating her for secondary syphilis. "And that little boy with the abscess on his head will need the dressing changed, but that's about it." I figured I could handle it as long as no emergencies turned up.

"I will be stopping in Ajoya to pick up some medical supplies. We are getting low on a few things. Is there anything you need?"

"If you see Stacy, could you pick up my camera and the ten rolls of film I left with her? And can you mail these letters for me?"

Ray took the letters. "I'll let Stacy know how well you are doing, too." For once, he smiled.

I was grateful that I had David Werner's book for reference. Fortunately for me, the next day was slow. Consuela and the little boy both stopped by. Other than that, I just saw a few skin rashes, so I was able to get all of my drawings and Halloween bags done.

On Halloween, I went to Victoria's for dinner and to see if she had found a pumpkin for me. "How's this one?" She held up a green and white round squash, not the bright orange pumpkin I was used to.

"It's perfect," I said, and we had great fun carving it.

When we were done, Victoria placed a candle inside and lit it. We both laughed at the spooky glow it cast in her kitchen. I couldn't wait to surprise my family with it.

Armed with a backpack full of candy bags, I walked through town on my way to Crecencio's, holding the pumpkin in front of me. The effect of its face glowing in the dark was fantastic. Curious people came out of their homes to take a look and the children squealed with delight. I handed out candy bags along the way.

Everyone at Crecencio's was in the kitchen talking. As I got closer to the house, I called out in English, "Trick or treat!"

My family ran out with excitement. I handed each one a bag of goodies. I dressed Verhenia with the paper pig nose, ears, and tail. She raced around making pig noises and everyone laughed.

Ilatio knew I played the guitar, so he left an old one for me at Crecencio's that day. While everyone was enjoying their treats, I played guitar and we sang *La Cucaracha.*

Afterwards, I taught them how to square dance, swinging each other round and round. It was a beautiful evening to be dancing outside. The stars were brighter than ever, and for the first time I noticed the flickering lights from fireflies. We were all punchy by the time we went to bed, exhausted from so much play and laughter.

This was by far the best Halloween I had ever celebrated. It made me feel good to be able to share something of my culture with these people who had already shared so much with me.

The next night, the kids begged me to light the pumpkin again. When I lifted up its top, about four thousand cockroaches came flying out! I screamed and jumped back in surprise. Everybody had a good laugh, and we enjoyed the lit-up pumpkin for one last time before the pigs got their chance to eat their Halloween Jack-O-Lantern treat.

Chapter 18
Dia de los Muertos

The next day at the clinic was a busy one. People from villages all around Chilar had come into town to celebrate *Dia de los Muertos.* Interestingly, a lot of them came to the clinic to meet me. They all wanted to tell me stories of past illnesses or ask questions about sick family members. It was sort of like an "Open House" at the clinic that day.

"It's difficult to give advice about patients without seeing them," I said with a smile. "You should bring them to the clinic."

Some showed me their old bullet wounds. Others showed where they were missing fingers from machete accidents. One man even wanted to show me his missing scrotum from a past gunshot wound. I swallowed hard and declined his generous offer.

It was late in the afternoon when, from the clinic, I noticed a procession forming on the other side of the river. People, all dressed in black, were walking up the narrow path to the cemetery. Women had black scarves covering their heads. They were carrying lighted candles and flowers to place on the graves of their loved ones. It was an eerie sight.

I decided to lock up the clinic and head back to town before it got too dark. I was much better at jumping the rocks across the river now and seldom fell in, but I preferred not to attempt it at night by flashlight.

Judging from the loud music I heard playing in the distance, the festivities had begun. It sounded like a record player. "That's odd," I thought, since there was no electricity in town.

When I got to my home, Ray was there. He had just ridden into town. "Here's a note from Stacy." It felt like Christmas. He pulled out my camera and film and a letter from my family. "The patient with malaria needed further evaluation, so I took him to Ajoya."

Ray had dinner with us - delicious tamales - then left for the clinic to drop off his bags and the medical supplies. "I'll be back shortly so we can go to the dance together."

While waiting, I eagerly read Stacy's note: *"I'm going to a remote clinic in the mountains. They say it will take two days to get there by mule. Want to come with me?"*

Sorry, Stacy . . . there was no way in hell I was going to take a two-day mule ride or any mule ride, for that matter! Later that week, I sent back a note wishing her the best of luck, and letting her know I was going to stay in Chilar.

I later heard that she only stayed a short time at that clinic, and then went home in December, much earlier than planned. I never found out why. Regretfully, we lost contact with each other and I never saw her again. It's funny how some people come into your life for a purpose and disappear once that purpose has been fulfilled. I felt like Stacy had come into my life to get me involved with Project Piaxtla and start me on my career path in medicine. I will always be extremely grateful to her.

I was just finishing up reading the letter from my parents when I heard Ray arrive. *"Vamanos."*

"Maria, would you like to join us?" She smiled and shook her head no. She said the dance was more for the younger people in town. I could tell her mind was made up, so we left without her.

As we walked to the schoolhouse where the dance was being held, we heard occasional gunshots in the distance. It worried me. Ray had told me days earlier that there was a feud between two families - one in Chilar and the other in a tiny village nearby. It had been a while since there was any fighting between them. I supposed the potential always existed, especially since there was bound to be alcohol and guns at the dance. *Please, no gunshot injuries tonight,* I prayed under my breath.

When we arrived, I noticed many unfamiliar faces, mostly men, mingling in the street drinking beer. Some were trying to look tough wearing their gun holsters. Young girls wore their best dresses and shoes with lots of makeup and red lipstick. Now I understood Maria's reluctance to come. The evening wasn't just about everyone dancing and enjoying themselves. It was about the younger men and women finding themselves a partner.

The record player was the old-fashioned kind that needed to be cranked before it could play. But it was really loud. They played the same record over and over again until the accordion and guitar players finally showed up, reeking of alcohol. They played for the rest of the evening and were actually quite good.

I was surprised at the formality of the evening. The girls sat in a line of chairs at one end of the dance floor and the men stood around at the other. If a man wanted to dance with a girl, he would stand in front of her and grab her hand. When the music started, he would lead her onto the floor and they would dance. After the music ended, he could either dance with her again, or lead her back to her seat and find a new available partner. It reminded me of a typical junior high dance.

Most of the time I just sat and watched with Ray, who didn't dance at all. I was asked to dance a few times by the older men. They asked me lots of questions: Did I like *cerveza*? Did I like to dance? Did I have a boyfriend back home? Was I married? Did I like Mexican men? It went on and on. I was just waiting for someone to ask me to "go up with him to the mountains." I'm sure they thought if they could just marry the *gringa,* (American woman) life would be perfect for them in the United States. Oh, if they only knew . . .

Esmeralda was there. A single mother, she brought her two teenage daughters to the dance and paraded them around in hopes of finding them a husband. They were heavily made up and looked scared and miserable.

Ray had his thoughts on Esmeralda. "Esmeralda supports her

girls by providing sexual favors to the men in town." He mentioned there was another single woman in Chilar, Rosaria, who did the same. She had five children from various fathers. It made sense now. I always thought a couple of her children looked a bit like Ilatio, the town mayor.

Ray continued to fill me in on other stories that night. I didn't know how much of it I should believe, considering the source. After all, Ray was someone who would be all smiles and compliments while we ate with a family, and then turn to me and say something demeaning about them or the meal they had prepared. He would say this in English so they would not understand.

By this time, I had grown used to Ray and his shortcomings. I personally found Ray to be two-faced, arrogant, and rather self-centered. I was itching for him to leave, but his departure was still three weeks off. His impressions of people were so different from mine. I decided it was time to focus on his good points. He had already been in Chilar for over six months and knew a lot of medicine. I would learn everything I could from him before he left, even if only through observation.

At midnight, we decided we'd had enough and left. At this point, girls were dancing with girls, laughing at the silliest things and having a great time. As we were leaving, out of the corner of my eye, I caught a hilarious sight. Miguel, a short and skinny man, was dancing with a large, fat woman. They were totally oblivious to this mismatch. How funny they looked together. They were so serious, concentrating intently on their dance steps.

Lying in my bed that night, I thought about what I had seen. I realized that beauty for these villagers came in all shapes and sizes, and they weren't nearly as conscious or judgmental about appearances as we were in the United States. Also, like children, they found joy and happiness in life's simple pleasures. I smiled and soon dropped off to sleep.

I got to the clinic the next morning and was relieved to discover that no one had been shot during the evening's festivities. A bullet dodged this time, so to speak, but I wouldn't be so lucky in the future.

Chapter 19

Consultas

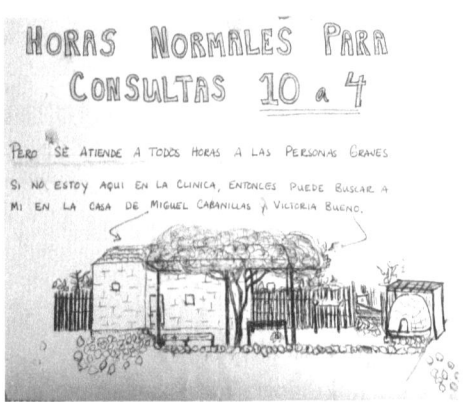

The week before the big dance, Ray and I attended a town meeting at the schoolhouse. That night the villagers agreed to pay for and install a cement floor at the clinic. We were very happy because it meant the community valued our presence. This would make a much cleaner, healthier environment for seeing patients. Ray had been asking for this for months, and he was pleased that it was finally going to happen before he left Chilar to return to the states.

Within a couple of weeks, we had a brand new cement floor in the clinic. Our examining table, chairs, and cot were finally level and we found it much easier to keep the floor clean. The clinic felt much more professional and sanitary.

With news spreading that there were two "medics" in Chilar,

people came from all over, even from long distances, for *consultas*.

My Spanish had improved significantly. Because I could understand and communicate (albeit with poor grammar) fairly well, I could now handle some of the easier *consultas* on my own. That helped on busy days. We saw a lot of the usual problems: colds and coughs, musculoskeletal strains and contusions, intestinal worms, skin problems, abscesses, and diarrhea, and vomiting.

Occasionally, we would see more challenging or interesting problems.

One mother brought in her four-year-old boy. His violent coughing spasms had a distinctive raspy sound, which I had never heard before. Ray recognized it right away. "Whooping cough."

We treated the child with erythromycin, an antibiotic. Then, using David's book, with its clear illustrations, I went over the contagiousness of the disease with the child's mother. "Keep your son away from other children if you can. Whooping cough spreads easily."

Another mother brought in her four-month-old infant who was losing hair, had some diarrhea, a cough and a skin rash all over his body. According to the mother, he was still breastfeeding okay. We were perplexed and couldn't find anything in David's book to guide us. The English medical text we had was mostly for adult illnesses.

Ray thought the child might have a vitamin deficiency and an infectious diarrhea. He started him on amoxicillin and vitamins, and told the mother to follow up in the Ajoya clinic. They left, never to be heard from again.

This was a common problem with many of the people we saw.

There was rarely any follow-up, so we didn't know if our treatments had been successful or not. I always prayed that we did more good than harm in these types of challenging cases.

Another time, I had just finished suturing up a young boy who had fallen and cut his head on a rock, when a middle-aged man came in complaining of pain in his bladder and frequent urination. He said he got it from a woman. We decided to treat him for both a urinary tract infection and for gonorrhea.

I was learning that venereal diseases were common in the Sierras for both men and women, since condoms weren't commonly used. I wondered why. Maybe it had to do with lack of availability, or lack of knowledge that condoms could prevent venereal diseases. I'm sure the macho mentality of Mexican men played a part, as did the Catholic Church, which counseled against all birth control methods.

Condom use would definitely have helped with our next patient, Ursula. Ray knew her well because she came in almost monthly to be treated for her vaginal infection. She claimed she had trichamonas and that she had been seen for it off and on for the past eight years. She went on to tell me that an injection of penicillin was the only thing that worked for her.

This was a commonly held belief by many in the Sierras: that an injection of penicillin was the best medicine for any of their ailments. They thought it was better than taking a pill. It always took a lot of effort and time to convince them otherwise.

When I wanted to examine Ursula she refused, saying she was on her period. Both Ray and I thought she couldn't keep having trichamonas all this time and wondered if there was a psychological component involved.

Ray gave her an injection, but of normal saline instead of the penicillin. He wanted to see how she would respond. She left the clinic content, having received an injection, unaware of the switch. I saw her in town the next day. "How are you doing, Ursula?"

"I'm cured!" She beamed.

Interesting. This was the first time I saw how a person's psyche played such an important role in their illness and treatment. It was an invaluable lesson that helped me care for patients throughout my medical career.

We never charged for *consultas* or expected anything in return, but many people felt compelled to give us gifts. Usually it was food: tamales, a couple of eggs, oranges, squash, or other garden produce. One time we got a live chicken. Ray decided we should make a chicken dinner for Francisco, Josephina, and their son.

What an ordeal that turned out to be! The hardest part was trying to kill the chicken. I had heard of killing a chicken by wringing its neck. I tried swinging it around by its neck, but the chicken just squawked and flapped its wings, irritated with me. I'm sure it was a couple of inches taller by the time I gave up. It was also still very much alive.

Ray finally found a dull knife and with difficulty cut its head off. I watched in horror as the bloody, headless torso jumped around for a little bit and then finally flopped over. After all this, I had completely lost my appetite. (And nearly lost my last meal as well!)

That evening, everyone choked down the overcooked chicken and rice meal we had prepared... except me. I couldn't bear to eat that poor chicken, and filled up on rice instead.

Months later, I received another young chicken as payment for a *consulta*. I gave it to Jeronima to raise with her chickens. She called it *La Mujer* (the woman) because none of the other chickens would mess with her as she strutted around the chicken coop, pecking at them if they got in her way. That chicken lived to be a ripe old age, and finally died of natural causes.

Chapter 20

A New Home

One morning, as I was getting ready to go to the clinic, I overheard Socorro and Crecencio talking about me. She was quite upset. She seemed to be saying how hard it was feeding another person in their already large household. I remembered Ray had originally asked them to put me up "temporarily," and it had already been over a month.

I jumped the rocks across the river and walked the steep, narrow trail to the clinic deep in thought. I was almost to the clinic when I stumbled and fell, catching myself with my left hand. That's when I noticed it. There on the ground, just inches away from my hand, was a huge black and orange tarantula. I got up quickly and bolted up the path. I had seen tarantulas in Chilar before, but never this close. Although I had been told they were not poisonous, this one, enormous and hairy, convinced me otherwise. I was sure it was deadly, and I would later write my parents telling them of my close brush with certain death.

I found Ray in the clinic checking a bottle of children's vitamins. "Look at this," he said. I could see the top of it had been partially chewed away. "It's the rats. They will chew through just about anything if they think there's food inside." The rats lived in the clinic rafters. You could hear them. Occasionally I saw their large black shadows scurrying around, especially when it got dark.

I had heard them in the rafters at Crecencio's house as well. Thankfully, they never bothered us. The only creatures that did were cockroaches and bedbugs, which, to my amazement, I had now become accustomed to.

I told Ray about the conversation I had overheard between Socorro and Crecencio. "It's time for me to find another place to live," I said. He agreed and offered to see if Francisco and Josephina would consider having me live with them.

While we were talking, two adult sons walked in with their frail and elderly mother. They said with some obvious embarrassment she had something "falling out" of her, and could we please help her. They added that it was getting so bad that she couldn't walk very far or ride a mule anymore. She was also beginning to have some problems with urination. They laid her down on the cot, and I examined her. I was shocked. More than half of her uterus was hanging out of her vagina! Not only this, but her cervix looked irregular and was extremely hard to the touch.

I told Ray what I found, and we concluded she probably needed a hysterectomy.

Ray turned to the young men. "You need to take her to the hospital. The closest one is in Culiacan. We can't do anything for her here."

They discussed this briefly with their mother, and quickly came to a decision. They would leave immediately for Culiacan. They had already walked some ten miles from their village, taking turns carrying their mother on their backs. Now they would have to carry her an additional five or six hours to Ajoya. From there they could take public transportation to Culiacan.

They had a long and difficult journey ahead of them. Yet, there was no hesitation or complaints from them. They knew it needed to be done, and they would just do it.

As I watched them leave, carrying their mother down the path, I pondered how many times I considered my life difficult. My challenges were nothing compared to what these people had to endure. This was yet another example of the villagers' resilience and problem-solving abilities. These examples of simple determination helped me put my own troubles in perspective. They made me realize how much I had to be grateful for, a life lesson that has served me well up until this very day.

I remembered I had promised Victoria I would bring her some shampoo for her dandruff and steroid cream for her rash. I also was going to help Maria wash clothes and take the kids bathing. "Ray, I have some things I need to do. I probably won't be back here today."

"Ok, I'll talk with Francisco about your living situation and get back to you."

When I got to Victoria's, I found her in the back yard picking chilies and tomatoes with Jeronima. She had a beautiful garden. Besides the vegetables, she had loads of flowers and fruit trees - mangos, lemons, and oranges.

I brought out the shampoo and cream and explained to her how to use each one. She thanked me, and invited me to stay for lunch.

The three of us sat around the table eating tortillas, refried beans and tomatoes. They both ate the hot chilies, but I declined. I had tried a small bite once before, and my mouth was on fire for days. They thought it was hilarious that I couldn't tolerate the chilies that they ate like candy.

Jeronima had something to ask me. "How much longer will you stay at Crecencio's?"

"Well, actually I hope to move out soon. It is really hard on them to have an extra mouth to feed all the time. Ray is going to ask Francisco if I can stay with them."

Victoria and Jeronima looked at each other. Victoria spoke first. "Why don't you move in with me and my family?" Jeronima added that she would have invited me to stay with her, but Victoria's house was much nicer.

"Oh, that would be wonderful. I'd love to!" I thanked her profusely. I was relieved I had a place to live, and excited that it was with Victoria. And Jeronima was just next door. I could move in the next day if I wanted.

Before I left, I bought some oatmeal and coffee from Victoria's general store. I wanted a gift to show my gratitude to Socorro and Crecencio for letting me stay with their wonderful family. When I got back to Crecencio's, Maria was collecting the laundry. I brought mine along, and we went down to the river with the kids in tow. I also brought my soap and shampoo to give them their weekly baths. I wondered if we'd still be doing this when I moved in with Victoria.

Ray found me by the river. "Francisco had just left when I got there. He'll be back tomorrow. I will ask him then."

"You won't have to," I said. " I just got an invitation to live with Victoria!" I was pretty excited. "I'll be moving in tomorrow." He seemed a little perturbed that I had taken matters into my own hands, but I also sensed that he was glad the problem was solved.

Later that evening, I sat down with all my first Chilar family and told them my plans. "I'll be moving to Victoria's house tomorrow. You have all been so wonderful to me. I will surely miss you." Soccoro looked relieved, but the rest of the family seemed sad. "Thank you so much for letting me stay with you for so long." I thanked them for their generous hospitality and gave them the oatmeal, coffee, and some money. At first they refused everything, but when I insisted, they finally agreed to take the food items. They simply would not accept the money. There were no hard feelings.

I remained good friends with Maria and the children, and they invited me to eat with them from time to time. Maria even embroidered some beautiful tablecloths for me. I still have them - a labor of love.

That next morning after a solemn breakfast, I gave them all hugs. With tears in my eyes, I waved goodbye. Crecencio helped me carry my belongings to my new home, where Victoria had a cot waiting for me.

Chapter 21

Thanksgiving

Eating Homegrown Honey in Rincon

The first night at Victoria's, I hardly slept a wink. A group of drunken men were playing the *consola* (music player) as loud as they could until the early morning hours. Victoria's house was in the middle of town, and they must have had the speakers aimed our way. I rarely heard the music when I stayed at Crecencio's, and when I did, it was not nearly as loud. He lived in the lower part of town, which I came to realize was the poorer, less rowdy section of Chilar.

    We slept in one large room. The four of them had the large cot at one end of the room, and I slept in a smaller one at the other.

Although I missed seeing Maria and all the kids at Crecencio's, I have to admit the smaller family and larger house was a welcome change.

When I got up the next morning, the kitchen was bustling with activity. Angel ground corn. Jeronima and her aunt, Sonia, visiting from out of town, made fresh tortillas, while Victoria cooked the beans. Soon, Celia and Manuel came in with more wood for the stove.

"Buenos dias," I said, as I walked in, rubbing my eyes. In unison, everyone looked up, smiled, and greeted me.

They were all talking about the loud music from the night before. Jeronima was irate. "I didn't sleep well at all," she said.

Victoria said the music didn't bother her. "The music was OK, but Celia kept pigging the bed!" Victoria turned to me. "Ilatio recently had a generator and phonograph brought in by mule. Now the drunks can play the *consola* all night." That explained the increased volume, too.

Life was much quieter and calmer in this home, and we had great conversations at mealtime. Victoria was a natural teacher, and under her tutelage my Spanish pronunciation and grammar improved immensely.

Another benefit of living here was getting to know Jeronima. It seemed she was always at Victoria's helping her with meal preparation and other chores. I noticed she was a hard worker and made sure everyone else was served before her. She was always the last to sit down and eat.

What I appreciated most about Jeronima was her great outlook despite having had such a hard life. Evidently her husband had left her years ago, and except for one daughter, all of her children had passed away. Her daughter lived in a distant village and visited Jeronima only a couple of times a year.

Her generosity amazed me. One day she took me to an unfamiliar small, run-down shack. She was bringing food to the elderly sister and brother who lived there: Ramalda, about eighty years old, and Don Pio, who, I was told, was close to a hundred. They relied on the goodness of the people of Chilar to take care of them. Jeronima probably watched after them the most. She had a big heart.

When we visited, I was surprised at how sharp Don Pio and Ramalda were. He could still walk short distances using a sturdy stick for support. Over the next couple of months, I too would visit with them, until I heard that Don Pio had passed away. Ramalda then left to live with relatives in another village.

One day shortly after my move, Ray announced, "I'm leaving soon. I need to get back and finish my pre-med studies. I do want to get into medical school." It was a sad day for the villagers, and for me, when he left. Despite our many differences, I relied heavily on his medical experience.

Now, if David allowed it, I would be running the clinic. I was feeling overwhelmed, but had to remember how much I had learned. The Ajoya clinic and their medical help was nearby if I needed it.

My plan was to return to Ajoya for more training. While there, we planned to celebrate Thanksgiving with a meal that Kerry, the lovely

Quaker woman from Colorado, would prepare for the volunteers. I dreaded the long trip on the back of a mule. My backside had not forgotten the nightmarish trip with Ray six weeks before. It would be my first time on a mule since I arrived in early October.

Victoria knew my fear of riding mules. She made some arrangements. "Miguel can take you. He will find the best mule for you to ride. And he'll watch out for you, too."

Miguel needed to go to Ajoya anyway to pick up merchandise for her store. With the help of Angel and Manuel, they would take a couple of donkeys and mules with them.

One day, shortly before I left for Ajoya, Victoria took me aside. "A few of the women are going to Rincon for some honey. It's not far. Would you like to join us?"

Rincon consisted of five or six homes occupied by two families. A beekeeper lived there and kept several hives. We had recently treated a woman from Rincon who suffered bad grease burns on both arms.

"I would love to join you," I said. "I need to check on a patient there anyway." I got some dressings and supplies in case I needed them, and we set off. I was happy to see Maria was part of the group, which gave us an opportunity to visit.

The walk was lovely, through a green valley dotted with mango, lemon, and orange trees. When we arrived, Victoria and I first checked in on the woman with the burns. She was healing nicely, and I only needed to bandage a small area that was still open. I left her with some dressings, and then the group of us went to the beekeeper's home.

We sat on the ground beside the hives as he opened one. With a smoky stick, he kept the bees at bay while he cut off a piece of honeycomb full of honey for each of us. I noticed everyone eating it, honeycomb and all. I tried a few bites, but it was way too sweet for me. We stayed for about an hour and left. Several of the women brought honeycombs home that day.

I guess something about that honey did not agree with me. I don't know what happened, but that night I got really sick with vomiting and diarrhea. I wasn't as ill as the first time. What made it exceptionally bad was all night long, unable to make it to the regular bathroom area, I blessed Victoria's garden with all kinds of fertilizer! The next morning, for the first time ever, I noticed Victoria letting a pig in to clean up. Normally, pigs were never allowed in that area. It was so embarrassing.

Thankfully, I was well enough for the trip to Ajoya a couple of days later. Miguel put me on a very gentle mule and watched after me the entire trip. Angel and Manuel walked and rode the donkeys off and on.

We traveled a more direct route, and this time it only took five hours to reach Ajoya. I was so relieved. I couldn't believe how easy and actually enjoyable the ride was.

Miguel took me to the clinic. Mike and Kerry came out to greet me, and grabbed my small bag. I thanked Miguel profusely, hugged him, and told him I'd see him in Chilar in a few days.

The next day we enjoyed Kerry's wonderful Thanksgiving meal with turkey and all the trimmings. We even had apple pie! We invited some locals to share the meal with us, but I'm afraid they didn't enjoy it as much as we did.

My time in Ajoya was very productive. I got the training I

needed from the dentist and felt prepared now to pull teeth. I also got needed medical supplies together to take back with me.

I had a chance to talk with David. "Now that Ray is leaving, will I be continuing in Chilar alone?"

"Are you okay with that?"

"It will be a big challenge," I said, "but I think I'm ready."

To my relief, David agreed.

Miguel on our way to Ajoya

Chapter 22
A Big Step Forward

My stay in Ajoya was cut short when Trinidad raced down from Chilar to get me. "Katalina, my daughter, Socorro, is hemorrhaging. You must come." He was breathless. "Socorro was skinning a snake. When she opened it up, she found two partially eaten rats." I recoiled at the thought.

Trinidad went on. "This created *susto* (frightened her) so much that she started to hemorrhage. She also just started her period."

I was skeptical, but Trinidad's urgent pleas could not be ignored.

"Okay, let's get back to Chilar." I grabbed my bags and medicines. I stopped long enough to ask advice from Kerry and Mike regarding this case. They suggested Ergotrate to stop the hemorrhaging.

They gave me one of the clinic's mules to ride. The mule was so slow Trinidad gave me one of his spurs and showed me how to use it. That did the trick. We trotted the whole way and arrived in Chilar in under five hours. I thought my body would be a wreck by the time I got there, but to my surprise I wasn't even sore.

When I saw Socorro, she looked pale and frightened, and the family was in a panic. I calmly sat down beside her, took out my stethoscope and blood pressure cuff and examined her as best I could. Martina, her mother, would not allow me to do a pelvic exam. Per Mike and Kerry's instructions, I injected her with Ergotrate (a drug used to stop hemorrhages after deliveries.)

I held her hand. "Socorro, you are going to be just fine. No, you're not going to die." After everyone calmed down, she finally went to sleep. Her vitals continued to be stable, so I left.

I visited her twice the next day. She seemed a little better; at least the bleeding had stopped. From time to time she would have these weird episodes of *susto*, rocking back and forth and repeating *Dios mio*. (My God)

I gave her some iron pills. "Take these. And try to eat more foods rich in iron." Turning to her parents I said, "More iron might help her to not bleed as much."

I eventually surmised she was having these *susto* attacks so that she wouldn't have to do any chores. She also hoped I'd have to visit her more often. I found out later she really liked me and this was her attempt to get me to live with her and her family.

When this became clear, I sat down with her and we had a long conversation. She did admit this was her motivation. I reassured her that although I wouldn't be living with her and her family, I would visit often. Miraculously, she was cured after that.

Looking back on the experience, I realized Socorro was probably having a heavier than normal menses, as young women her age did from time to time. Because of superstitions and hysterical tendencies, the family thought it was more.

The villagers of Chilar held lots of other odd beliefs and superstitions. For example, it was considered *hace dano* (bad for you) to eat any citrus fruit when one had *agripe* (a cold.) Other beliefs forbade a woman who had just given birth from bathing for one week. She was not to eat meat for a full month after the delivery either. No matter how often I told them that these beliefs were not true, many remained unconvinced.

    I was happy the situation with Socorro had ended well. I felt that I had taken a giant step forward in my medical journey. I was able to calmly assess the situation, looking for possible non-medical solutions. I gained the family's confidence as well as their respect.

Chapter 23
Crecencio Pena

Life seemed to settle down into a routine. I enjoyed spending mornings with Victoria and Jeronima. They corrected my Spanish and taught me to make delicious Mexican food. I hurried off to the clinic by ten o'clock and stayed until five, Monday through Friday. I had the weekends to myself unless somebody found me, wanting a *consulta*.

It seemed that most of the medical care I provided was handing out cough medicine, de-worming medicine, or pain medicine - mostly aspirin for aches and strains. I treated a lot of skin infections as well.

One mother brought her twelve-year-old daughter up because she had tummy aches. While I was asking questions, the girl vomited and out came an intestinal worm. Later, she vomited so hard another worm came out, but through her left nostril. The mother calmly grabbed it and pulled it from her nose.

I was shocked. I had never seen anything like this before. The mother and daughter didn't seem to be upset at all. At least I now knew the source of her tummy aches, and sent them home with de-worming medicine.

In general, the clinic wasn't terribly busy. *Consultas* seemed to come in spurts, so I could spend time studying medicine and the drugs we had on our shelves. I was also able to write long letters to family and friends.

One day on my way to the clinic, I noticed a new face in town. He was a handsome young man about my age. His eyes followed me the entire length of the street. When I got close, I smiled and said, *"Buenos dias."* He smiled back and returned the greeting.

It wasn't long before he surprised me at the clinic. "I am Crecencio Pena, and I have come for a *consulta.*"

"What kind of problems are you having?" He didn't look very sick.

"I have a terrible pain." His brown eyes looked straight at me.

"Where is the pain?" Without a word, he pointed to his heart.

"How long have you had it?"

With deep sincerity, he answered, "Ever since I laid eyes on you." *Oh, brother,* I thought, *another Mexican man trying to hit on me.*

I laughed. "You had better go take a cold bath in the river. That will surely help."

Fortunately, at that moment, another person needing medical attention interrupted us. I told Crecencio there was nothing more I could do for him, so he left. I shook my head in disgust, amazed at his forward approach, thinking these men will try anything!

Later at Victoria's I recounted the story. "You won't believe what happened today."

Victoria laughed. "Crecencio has just returned from Los Angeles to help his family with their farm. He is really very nice. He doesn't smoke or drink to excess, like his brother." She told me a story in which Crecencio's brother was drunk one night, beating his wife, and Crecencio had stopped him, holding him back with tears in his eyes. Evidently he had to do this many times.

He did sound like a nice guy. Victoria hinted what a great boyfriend he would make for me. After our first encounter, however, I was not impressed and certainly not interested.

Every so often I would see him in town and we would talk, or he'd occasionally come up to the clinic to visit. At the dances, he always asked me to dance. He was a gentleman and he had such kind eyes.

As I got to know him better, I started to like him more and I enjoyed his company. One time he accompanied Victoria, Miguel, and me to a small village an hour away by mule. We had been invited to eat a pig. It was a lot of fun and Crecencio was very careful to make sure I was comfortable on the mule, helping me on and off.

Some nights we'd go for walks. It was so lovely and romantic under the bright stars with the fireflies blinking.

Eventually, yes, to the delight of the entire town, we did become *novios* (boyfriend, girlfriend).

I remember sitting outside of Victoria's house looking across the river when he would tell me how he could build me a house in that clearing. He'd work on the farm, bringing home food, and I could continue working at the clinic, and we'd eventually have children. He was a bit of a dreamer.

These conversations always made me very uncomfortable. It all sounded so romantic. I even wondered if I could live in Chilar permanently. But I knew that I wanted to go back to school and become a nurse. Deep down inside, I knew this relationship could never succeed.

In March 1975, a month before I was to leave Chilar to return home, the town's mayor, Ilatio, came to see me. "Katalina, Crecencio has sent me to ask you a question."

"And what might that be?" I wondered why he didn't just ask me himself.

"He wants to ask for your hand in marriage and he sent me." Whoa! This certainly took me by surprise. I took a deep breath.

"Ilatio, please ask Crecencio to come see me after he returns from his *milpa*."

Later that afternoon, Crecencio found me. Holding his hand, I tried to let him down gently. "I care for you very much. You are a very good friend and a wonderful person." His eyes looked hopeful. "But our backgrounds are so very different. Our goals in life are not at all the same." He looked down at the ground. "Crecencio, I can't marry you. I couldn't live in Chilar my whole life."

Naturally, he was hurt. That was the end of our relationship. He did, however, come up to California a couple of years later to find me, wanting to rekindle our relationship. We did meet several times, but things had changed too much and it didn't work out.

    I often wonder where he is living now, and if he ever married and had children.

Chapter 24
Caballo de Arriba

While going through the medicines in the clinic one morning, I heard some mules pull up outside. I walked out to find a man with an empty mule beside him, all saddled up and ready to go. "Can you help me? My friend shot himself in the leg four days ago. It was an accident."

I assumed alcohol was probably involved. "Where do you live?"
"We live in Caballo de Arriba."

"Where's that?" I asked. He pointed to a distant mountain range.

Without thinking much about the mule ride, I grabbed some surgical soap, dressing changes, and penicillin. I locked the clinic and went to Victoria's to pack a small bag of clothes to take with me. "I'm headed to Caballo de Arriba."

When I told her where I was going, she looked very concerned. "Katalina, the ride to Caballo is very long and very dangerous."

Part of me thought it couldn't be any worse than my first mule ride with Ray into Chilar. Well, I was wrong! It was worse. The only difference was this guide knew what he was doing. He didn't seem bothered by the trip, which kept me calm for most of the journey.

Still, there were moments when I was terrified and my mouth was completely dry. We had to ride over two and a half mountain ranges. At a couple of places along the way, we had to get off our mules to walk because the path was either too narrow or too steep. In another area, we rode our mules along a narrow cliff that hugged the side of the mountain with a hundred foot drop to the river on the other side. I prayed the whole time that my mule wouldn't stumble. I held on tight.

When I looked up at my guide, he appeared to be dozing in his saddle. I couldn't believe it. Didn't he see what danger we were in?

At one point I was so terrified I became angry with God, saying, "You brought me all this way to die on a mule!" It was then and there that I accepted my death. By coming to this realization, I had in effect accepted my life and a big weight was lifted off of me. Somehow, I knew I was going to be okay.

We arrived in Caballo de Arriba at sunset, six hours later. It was freezing. After all, it was December and this village was much higher in elevation than Chilar. I noticed how primitive and bleak the town was. Since they had no kerosene lamps, they used pinewood torches for light.

They also built a huge bonfire at night and in the morning for warmth. They took me to the patient who was lying on a cot in an open-air room.

A few of the villagers with their children were there as well. They had come to see the *"Americana."* I got the feeling that for some of them, this was the first time they had ever seen a white person. As a matter of fact, a couple of the children came up and touched my face to see if the white would rub off.

When I examined the man's wound, I saw the bullet had entered through the inside of the left calf and exited out of the sole of the left foot. Both his leg and foot were so swollen it was hard for me to examine them to see if there was any bone involvement. At least he had full sensation in his leg and foot and could move his toes and ankles a little, but with pain.

The family taking care of him had been injecting him daily with penicillin so there was no sign of infection. (Believe it or not, it was not uncommon for remote villages to keep a supply of injectable penicillin, in case of emergency.) I cleaned his wound with surgical soap and dressed it. I had him put his leg up and told him to keep it elevated at all times. After eating, I went to bed wearing all my clothes, and I still froze most of the night.

In the morning, they built another bonfire for warmth, and I warmed up for the first time. For two days, I changed the dressing and gave the patient injections of penicillin daily.

During that time, many villagers and their children continued to visit. Evidently, I was their excitement for the week. Some invited me to their homes for meals. I also got a tour of the town, which consisted of eight or so wooden shacks that sat beside a raging river. The terrain was very rocky and bare. The houses were spread apart, some even as much as a quarter mile. One family invited me over to eat oranges. We had to walk along a narrow cliff to get there with a steep drop down to the river. Why these villagers chose to live in such a remote and treacherous area was beyond me.

The patient's swelling eventually went down, and the foot and leg were looking better. I showed the patient's family how to clean and dress the wound. "Keep his leg elevated as much as possible and continue giving him penicillin for another five days. He should really go to Ajoya for an X-ray to see if there's a fracture; he might need a cast." They didn't appear to want to do this. "There is nothing more I can do."

I needed to get back to Chilar. They made arrangements for me to leave the next day.

I was grateful the return trip to Chilar was not as scary as the ride out to Caballo de Arriba. I guess I knew what to expect and I had the same guide, who I trusted.

I had a whole new appreciation for Chilar, and was so glad to get back. Chilar was a warm paradise in comparison to Caballo de Arriba. Victoria greeted me with a hot meal, and we spent the rest of the evening talking about my experience in the Sierras. She couldn't believe what all I'd been through. She surprised me by heating water for a hot shower that night. What a thoughtful, loving treat. It was great to be home.

Chapter 25
Pulling teeth

I lay in bed one morning, excited. Today would be my first dental appointment... as the dentist! Esteban was coming to the clinic expecting me to pull a tooth. He had been suffering for two weeks, and the toothache was getting worse.

Jumping out of bed, I felt an immediate sting on the ball of my right foot. Ouch, that hurt! I grabbed my flashlight and went hunting for the culprit. There, underneath the cot, was a large scorpion. I killed it and showed it to Victoria. "Don't worry, that kind is not poisonous," she said.

What?! There was a poisonous kind? I had no idea there were two types of scorpions. She told me this type of scorpion gave a painful bite and would cause numbness and tingling for a couple of days in my foot and leg. Sure enough, over the next several hours, I could feel numbness and tingling spreading from my foot, up my leg, all the way to my mid thigh. It was a weird sensation trying to walk on a leg that was partially numb, and it caused me to limp. Fortunately, after two days, my symptoms cleared and everything was back to normal.

By the time I limped up to the clinic, Esteban was waiting for me. I looked in his mouth, and I could see a huge cavity in his right lower first molar. I'm not sure which one of us was more scared. I hid my nervousness and thought of my dad.

I took out my xylocaine, syringe, needle, and instruments and went to work. After I was able to get the jaw completely numb, I grabbed the tooth with my dental "pliers" and started to pull. It was really socked in there, and took all of my strength, rocking it back and forth, to finally get it out. We were both relieved when it was over. I couldn't wait to write home and tell my dad the dentist all about it.

"Rinse your mouth several times a day with warm salt water, and try not to get food in the area." I gave him some aspirin and some penicillin to take for a couple of days.

I must have pulled fifteen to twenty teeth during my months in Chilar. Poor oral hygiene and consumption of sugar, especially sugar cane, were the main causes for the many cavities. If the villagers had been near a proper dentist, they might have had the option to have their cavities filled and the teeth could have been saved. But in remote areas, extraction was the only solution to their painful toothaches. If they were not pulled, serious complications could result, like spreading abscesses and sepsis.

Once one of the villagers took me up to show me his sugar cane fields. He gave me a piece of sugar cane, and showed me how to chew it and suck the sugar out. It seemed like a lot of work to get a small amount of sugar, and I couldn't understand why this was such a treat for them. He showed me how they cut the cane stalks, and placed them in a press that was powered by a donkey pulling a lever going around in a circle. This would squeeze the sugar out of the cane, which they could then pour into wooden molds. Here it would solidify and become caked brown sugar, ready for consumption and more cavities.

Most of the time I didn't have any trouble pulling teeth. I

remember one man whose tooth was so rotten that when I pulled it, it came out in pieces. It took me quite a while to get it entirely out, root and all.

Then there was Ursula, the drama queen. She came to me that day, not for vaginal issues, like she had previously, but because of a bad toothache. She was terrified at the prospect of having it removed, but she couldn't suffer the pain any longer.

While I was getting my instruments ready, she was on the porch on her knees, with her hands in the air, praying loudly and passionately to Dios, to Jesus, and Mother Mary that they might help her and be by her side during her upcoming ordeal. It was almost comical to hear her go on and on in Spanish with her desperate pleas.

The extraction went smoothly, and there were no problems. I gave her the medicines, and she left to go home, happy it was over with and she survived.

Later than evening, when I went by her home to check on her, she was walking around with a white kerchief tied around her chin and head, holding her cheek with her hand, saying, *"Ay Dios, Ay Dios."* The numbing medicine had worn off, and she was in pain. She would stop every so often, spit saliva, and then start up again with *"Ay Dios, Ay Dios."*

She wanted to make sure that anyone who walked by knew how much she was suffering. It took her several days to recover, in contrast to my usual patients, who were fine the next day. Not surprisingly, she had no more teeth pulled after that.

Chapter 26
Christmas and New Years

Chilar Schoolhouse

The week before Christmas, Chilar was bustling with activity and excitement. Big meals were planned. Several pigs were killed, and women got together at various homes to prepare the Christmas feast.

The seamstress in town was busy with her old-fashioned foot pedal sewing machine making new dresses for many of the young girls. Victoria made sure her store was stocked with several different fabric bolts. She insisted that I have the seamstress make me a dress as well. The talented seamstress came to the house and took my measurements. Within two days the dress was ready and fit perfectly. It was a white fabric with small flowers, cut to above my knees, with short puffy sleeves. I felt like a princess!

It rained so much Christmas Eve and Christmas Day that the river was flooded and I couldn't get across to the clinic. Luckily, no one was seriously ill, and any on-going health concerns could wait until the flooding subsided.

Christmas was a different kind of celebration in Chilar. It was more like a huge festival with lots of beer drinking and shooting of guns.

This was also a busy time for the drunks who loved to play loud music every night on the phonograph, making it impossible for anyone to sleep. Occasionally, they would come up to Victoria's house in the early mornings demanding that Miguel open up the store and sell them cigarettes. After several nights of this, I finally went to Ilatio and complained. That did seem to help, for a while, anyway.

I vividly remember one night when three drunkards carried the

hand-held cranked phonograph in front of Victoria's place and played it as loud as they could. After an hour of this, I'd had it, and was raging mad. I got dressed, stomped outside and said, "We can't sleep. Turn off that music and go home."

The man who was the drunkest pulled out his gun, waved it in the air, and in slurred speech said, "Wha's the problem?"

With that, I replied, "Oh, there's no problem. That music is just delightful."

When he put his gun back in his holster, I slipped inside the house. Phew! That was a little scary! Fortunately, they left shortly after that.

On Christmas Eve, everyone packed into the schoolhouse to watch some of the villagers put on a Christmas play. The characters were all dressed as either angels or devils. The men had flowers in their sombreros and carried long poles decorated with flowers. At one point I recognized Mary, Joseph, and Baby Jesus but had no idea what was going on. I was surprised at all the noise and beer drinking amongst the audience. It was not exactly the holy, religious "Silent Night" experience I was accustomed to in the States.

After the play, the audience stayed in the schoolhouse because of the rain. They moved tables and chairs out of the way to make room for a dance floor. I surprised everyone by wearing my new dress. I felt like I probably danced with every man in the Sierras that night. That included Crecensio, who I was still getting acquainted with.

I made it clear to the men that I wouldn't dance with anyone who carried a gun. I was surprised how quickly they removed their holsters!

I danced until the early morning and must have been asked for my hand in marriage at least five or six times. All night long the drunks went outside and fired off their guns, startling everyone. I always shuddered when I heard the gunfire, praying that no one got hurt.

Before I went to bed that night, I drew a picture of Santa Claus and left it in the house with some cookies and candies for Victoria's family to find. When they saw it the next morning, it was a tremendous hit. We had a special Christmas feast, but I noticed no gifts were exchanged.

The week before New Year's I was busy with *consultas*. Of note was the man from Caballo de Arriba who shot himself in the leg. He was brought to Chilar on a stretcher. I was told before he came that he was much worse and was very ill. But when he arrived, he actually was much better. The wounds were healing nicely, and the swelling was nearly gone in his leg and foot. He was upset because his injured leg muscle was smaller than his other leg. I explained to him why this leg had atrophied and gave him exercises to do. I still wanted him to go to Ajoya for X-rays, but he refused.

"I can't go there." He seemed nervous. "I could be arrested in Ajoya."

"Why?"

"Because of my gun."

That's when I learned that guns were illegal, as was *cerveza*. Of course, in Chilar, with no local police force, people could do pretty much what they wanted. So they drank and fired their guns to their heart's content.

The man wanted me to 'fix' him in Chilar so he wouldn't have to risk repercussions in Ajoya for possessing a gun. I told him his wounds would heal, but I couldn't guarantee that he wouldn't be left with a bad limp from a weaker leg, or have to use crutches or a cane for the rest of his life.

When I went to check on him the next day, I discovered he had returned to Caballo. I'm sure he was frustrated that I couldn't fully and instantly heal him of his injury.

The New Year's Eve dance was held at Victoria's house on her veranda. A beautiful flowering bougainvillea spread over the dance floor. Once again, there was lots of *cerveza* and gunfire. I danced until three o'clock in the morning and received tons of marriage proposals.

Whenever Crecencio asked me to dance, all eyes were upon us. It was as if they thought we were already *novios* (boyfriend, girlfriend.)

At midnight, to welcome in the New Year, the men fired off their guns in unison for several minutes. One stray bullet managed to hit an owl sitting in the bougainvillea tree. It dropped dead on the dance floor, to everyone's surprise. Thankfully, that was the only casualty of the night.

Though it was my first Christmas away from my father and family, I was so fascinated with the celebration that I had little time to feel homesick. It was an interesting two weeks for me, celebrating the holidays "Chilar style."

Chapter 27

A Visit Back Home

I had written several letters to family and friends telling them I would be home in January for a short visit. I asked everyone to start collecting sweaters and clothing that I could bring back to Chilar with me. There were so many people in Chilar who could use warm clothing.

One woman in particular came to mind. She and her family had lived in another village when, six months earlier, for some ungodly reason, her brother shot and killed her husband, her mother, and two of her children. She fled that very day with her six remaining children to Chilar. The villagers helped her until she became established. Now she worked at various jobs to help support her family. I was going to make sure I brought back a piece of warm clothing for each one of them.

The day to travel back arrived and I went with Miguel and Angel to Ajoya. They were going to get supplies for the store. I was pleased at how comfortable I felt riding on mules now. Just three months earlier I swore I would never get used to this form of transportation. It looked like I wouldn't need that helicopter to rescue me from Chilar after all.

I stayed overnight in the Ajoya clinic, gathering up my guitar and my other belongings to take back with me. I had a great time talking with Kerry and Mike about our different medical cases and challenges.

For the next twenty-seven hours, sleeping intermittently, I took buses that finally got me to Tijuana. I then took a bus to San Diego, and another to Davis.

It was a serious culture shock for me when we crossed the border into the United States. I couldn't believe how clean it was, and how many nice cars were on the smooth interstate freeways. There were stores full of merchandise, gas stations at every corner and everyone was dressed so nicely. The first time I walked into a grocery store I was overcome by all of the food lining the shelves. Why hadn't I ever noticed this before?! We truly are a wealthy nation, and have more than we could ever need. It's too bad we can't distribute some of this wealth to those in need and end poverty once and for all.

I spent several days in Davis with my friend Nancy. She had received my applications for nursing school, so I completed them and sent them in. She also received a small box of toothbrushes and toothpaste that Colgate had sent me as a donation. I was able to see a few friends and gather some clothing to bring back with me to Chilar.

Then I spent several days with my family in Terra Linda. They had been able to collect clothing from neighbors for me as well.

Although it was great seeing my family and friends, it felt surreal. My thoughts and my heart were still in Chilar, and I was anxious to get back. I was afraid that I would lose what Spanish I had gained if I stayed too long speaking only English, and I found myself missing everyone tremendously.

After ten days, I said goodbye to my family and friends and headed back to Mexico on a bus. I had a large rucksack filled with all the warm clothing I'd collected.

When I crossed the border, a border officer examined my bags. He found my box of toothbrushes and toothpaste, as well as the rucksack full of clothes.

When he saw all this, he cleared his throat, puffed out his chest and started in. "You must pay if you want to bring these items into our country. Just give me twenty American dollars, and it is okay."

I was furious. "Why? I am bringing these things for needy people in the Sierras of Sinaloa. I will not pay you a bribe." I said all this in flawless Spanish. I think he was amazed that I spoke so well and that I knew what he was doing was illegal. He quickly let me through without any further harassment.

The remainder of the long trip was uneventful. When I finally got to Ajoya, I had to wait around for three days until somebody could send down a mule and a burro to get me back to Chilar.

I spent some time seeing patients with Mike and Kerry in the clinic, but I was anxious to get back. Finally my transportation and my guide arrived. I loaded the burro with my bulging bags and mounted the mule.

I was so excited when we rounded the corner and I saw the corral into which Super Mule had galloped months earlier when I first arrived at Chilar.

No one knew I was going to arrive that day, so they were surprised and happy to see me. Crecencio and Socorro, as well as several other families, invited me to stay with them. I thanked them profusely, but told them I would be going back to Victoria's again.

That night the villagers celebrated my return by playing music on the phonograph. They all came by to see me and hear about my trip home.

It was a wonderful welcome home, and I felt very much loved and accepted.

Chapter 28

My Birthday Celebration

Back in Chilar, I distributed the warm clothing to those most in need, including the woman with six children. Everyone was so humble and grateful for the clothes I brought them. I gave Jeronima a warm ski sweater that she wore almost constantly that winter.

I took a group of children to the river to bathe, gave them each their own toothbrush and toothpaste, and showed them how to brush correctly. I had enough left over that I was able to give toothbrushes and toothpaste with instructions to other families who had lots of children.

I realized all of this was probably going to make no more than a tiny dent in the great need that existed, but at least it was a start.

The next day, I was in the clinic when I saw Jose, a young boy with a tender abscess on the top of his foot. "I stepped on a stick about a month ago. I thought I pulled it all out." But in the past week, he noticed a small bump forming on the top of his foot. What had happened was a piece of the wood was still in his foot, and it was slowly making its way to the surface.

I numbed the area and lanced the abscess. In the process of irrigating and cleaning the area, a half inch piece of wood popped out. *All right!* This was very satisfying because I couldn't always locate foreign bodies on my first attempt to remove them. It sometimes took days for the foreign body to come to the surface, where I could remove it. After thoroughly cleaning the wound, I loosely sutured it and wrapped it in gauze. I also put him on some penicillin for seven days.

I checked on him over the next several days, and the wound remained clean and was healing nicely. I took the sutures out in ten days, and he was completely healed.

Word got out that my birthday was the 10th of February, so Victoria and Jeronima killed a chicken for a special meal and arranged for a dance. I couldn't believe what a big deal everyone was making of this, but I had to admit I was enjoying all of the attention. Maria, from my first Chilar family, gave me material for another dress. The village dressmaker took my measurements and I told her how I wanted the dress to look. Within four hours she had finished it, and it was a perfect fit.

At five o'clock on the morning of my birthday, I woke up to music. Esteben and Crecencio, knowing they had to be in their *milpas* by six o'clock, rose early to sing me happy birthday. All day long music was played in my honor, and an announcement was made that it was the Americana Katalina's birthday, and that there would be a dance that evening.

That night on Victoria's veranda under the bougainvillea we celebrated. I wore my new dress and got lots of compliments. Everyone knew that I wouldn't allow guns or shooting, so all we heard that night was music from the accordion player and his guitarist and lots of singing.

By this time, Crecencio and I were an "item" and we were seeing a lot of each other. We danced the night away. The other men teased me and asked when we were going to get married, settle down, and have children in Chilar. I just smiled.

I noticed Victoria spent a lot of time talking to the musicians, especially the accordion player, but I didn't think anything of it.

At one point they brought out a cake with candles on it, and sang happy birthday to me in Spanish. What fun! It was so special to be surrounded by wonderful friends celebrating under the stars in the mountains of Sinaloa on my special day. I was happy to see everybody enjoying themselves, and I was so grateful for all of their good wishes. It will always be one of my most memorable birthday celebrations ever.

Chapter 29
Ernesto's Godparents

I was on my way to the clinic one morning when Pablo chased me down. "Please come, Katalina. My daughter, Rita, she's very sick."

She was having terrible abdominal pain along with vomiting since early that morning.

When I walked in, she looked very pale. When I examined her and I touched her right lower quadrant, she had severe pain. All of the symptoms and signs pointed to appendicitis.

"I think we need to take her to Ajoya. Can you find some men and make a stretcher? We have to hurry. She might need surgery."

Within a couple of hours, Rita was on a makeshift stretcher. Two volunteers carried her and several others went along, either on foot or mule waiting to relieve them. I was happy to see that my friend Crecencio was one of them.

I rode on a mule the entire distance, checking on Rita from time to time. Amazingly we arrived in Ajoya in four hours. Mike and Kerry were at the clinic and placed Rita on an examining table. I gave them the history and Mike examined her thoroughly.

"She doesn't seem nearly as sick as when we left Chilar," I said. I was surprised that her abdomen was not as tender in the right lower quadrant as before. Mike decided to give her some IV fluids of normal saline and an anti-nausea medicine. I was scratching my head. I thought appendicitis was a medical emergency and always required surgery.

"What do you think, Mike?"

He surmised that perhaps an intestinal worm lodged itself in the blind sac of the appendix, causing inflammation, nausea, vomiting, and acute right lower quadrant pain. At some time during the trip, the worm must have squirmed out of the appendix so it was no longer inflamed.

"We can keep her here and watch for improvement. If the symptoms return, we'll transport her immediately to a hospital in Culiacan for an appendectomy." I was relieved that Rita was feeling better. Her dad decided to stay with her. Other volunteers elected to spend the night as well, and return to Chilar the next day.

Crecencio and I had to get back to Chilar for a ceremony we were going to be involved in. We had been asked to be the godparents of Crecencio's two-year-old nephew, Ernesto. Fortunately, it was early enough for us to make the mule ride back that day. Two other volunteers returned with us. The ride was beautiful. Along the way, we witnessed a lovely sunset and watched the stars slowly begin to shine brighter and brighter in the night sky, millions of them. En route, Crecencio and the other two volunteers started singing some of their favorite Spanish songs. They all had gorgeous voices, which just added to the magic of the evening.

We didn't get back until later that night. I was exhausted and slept deeply, grateful that everything had turned out well. The next morning after breakfast, I put on my dress. Victoria and Jeronima also dressed up for the ceremony.

We walked to the house of Ernesto's parents, Rufina and Nito (Crecencio's brother.) Here Crecencio and some of the other villagers met us. Maria gave me a scarf to put on my head and then we all went to the river. It seemed like everybody in Chilar was there to witness the ceremony.

First we lit a candle together. Crecencio read a verse from a booklet, which I repeated. We each did this three times. Then Crecencio lifted up Ernesto, who was crying the whole time, and handed him to Rufina and then recited another verse. Essentially this verse announced: "Crecencio and Katalina are godparents in the eyes of God." Then it was my turn to lift up Ernesto and hand him to Nito, reciting the same verse. It was a very touching and beautiful ceremony. Afterwards, we went back to Nito's house and had coffee and cookies.

I still wonder to this day whatever happened to my godson, Ernesto. I'm sorry I didn't keep in touch with him over the years.

Chapter 30
Unusual Labor and Deliveries

Socorro and her baby

Generally, it was the custom in Chilar for pregnant women in labor to call a midwife. Oflacia, an older woman from a village called Borbontita, was a self-taught *partera* (midwife). Although she lived two and a half hours away, everyone called her. They trusted her. This was a relief to me, because I had no training in labor and delivery. I prayed I would not be called upon to help deliver babies.

I attended only one of Oflacia's deliveries, and it was complicated. One of the women in town was having a difficult breech labor. I watched in horror as Oflacia, without washing her hands or putting on gloves, put both hands into the pregnant woman's vagina and started yanking on the infant's trunk. The woman screamed in pain. I cringed inside; it looked so brutal.

Finally, with a squishing sound, an infant with a large head was delivered dead. On closer examination, the head was not only large, but also wobbly and full of fluid. As soon as this baby was delivered, another head appeared and a normal baby girl was delivered without difficulty. I actually helped with this twin's delivery and cut the umbilical cord. Then both placentas came out without any problem.

It was interesting that in this set of twins, one was obviously very abnormal. I had never seen anything like this and didn't know what may have caused it. Was this just an abnormal fetus, or the result of such a forceful delivery? I chose to believe it was an abnormal fetus, and that it would not have survived even in the best of circumstances.

Just a week before I was to leave for the United States, Pancho's wife Socorro gave birth to a baby boy, using the same midwife. The midwife used pitocin freely during Socorro's exceptionally long labor.

The baby was delivered normally, but the placenta did not follow. I wondered if this might be because of the liberal and extensive use of pitocin. This drug is used to help start labor by causing uterine contractions and can also help with bleeding.

Socorro was not feeling well following the birth. Pancho came to get me.

I had been washing clothes by the side of the river when a goat got hold of my powdered detergent and started to eat it. I had no idea goats could digest such things. They were worse than pigs. I was chasing the goat so I could retrieve my bag when Poncho waved me down.

"Socorro just delivered the baby, but she looks pale. Something is not right. Will you come?" I ran to the clinic, got my blood pressure cuff, thermometer and other items, and ran straight to his house. I also brought my obstetrics book.

I checked Socorro's blood pressure. It was very low and her pulse was over one hundred. I was worried that she was losing blood behind the retained placenta.

"Pancho, can you go to Ajoya right away and get some help?"

I wrote a note to Mike and Kerry explaining the situation and gave it to Pancho. He left right away.

I felt I aged thirty years that night. I was so afraid Socorro was going to die on me. All night long, I stayed by her side, checking her vitals. I couldn't find anything in the OB book on treatment of retained placenta.

After several hours, I decided to start an IV on her. I had done only one IV in my life, but at least I had watched many being done. I put on the tourniquet and got a blood vessel to pop up. After swabbing it with alcohol, I took a deep breath and stuck the needle in, and got it in on the first try. What a relief! I hooked her up to the IV solution and waited.

Finally, I saw Pancho galloping up with a box hanging on the saddle horn, but no one had come with him. My heart sank.

I was exhausted. I was in way over my head. I was hoping for another medical person to come up and take over. Instead, I got a box of instructions and supplies. I read the note from Mike: *"You're doing a good job. Continue the IV fluid, but add penicillin and iron."*

In another hour, her vitals were beginning to look better. When that liter was done, I hooked up another one, and gave her the antibiotics and iron per the instructions. Thankfully, her vitals continued to improve.

Many villagers stopped by to see how she was doing. Even in her weakened state, she talked to everyone. She was a courageous, caring, and strong woman. She always wanted to make sure everyone who visited had something to eat or drink and was comfortable.

I told Carmelita, her teenage daughter, to continue to give her water by mouth, while I went back to my house to eat and take a nap.

I had probably been asleep for an hour when they woke me up, very happy and excited. Socorro had passed the placenta and thankfully there was not a lot of bleeding.

When I walked into her room, Socorro was sitting up, talking, and had some color in her face. She looked so much better. She was even breastfeeding her baby. My terrifying experience was at an end.

Thankfully, mother and baby came through just fine.

Chapter 31
Jeronima

Victoria was gone. She took off with the accordion player, leaving behind her two children and Miguel. I couldn't believe it. There was absolutely no indication that she was going to do this. I knew she didn't really love Miguel and that she used him for her own selfish purposes, but still I had no idea this was going on with the accordion player. Evidently, they had left early that morning.

"Victoria left?" Jeronima was as shocked as I was. She took one look at my face and made a decision. "You will move in with me." She fixed up a cot for me and put all of my belongings on the shelf near it.

Two days later Victoria sent for her two children. She was now living in a village four hours away with the accordion player. Miguel was brokenhearted. Angel, her brother, had already gone to stay with his father in a different village. Miguel eventually closed the store and he, too, left Chilar.

I was excited and pleased that Jeromina insisted I live with her. I knew I could have stayed with any of several other families, but I really preferred being with Jeronima. We had become good friends, and she had so much to teach me.

During my last six weeks in Chilar, Jeronima sometimes took me to the mountains and showed me some of the medicinal herbs that were

commonly used for things like fevers, infections, and skin rashes. We gathered wood together and sometimes take her cows to graze in nearby valleys rich with green grass. She showed me how to milk a cow and how to feed the chickens.

Jeronima was a remarkable woman and she was a bit like a mother to me. "Would you ever consider going to America to live with me?" I asked her once.

She never wanted to go, saying that she belonged in Chilar.

"I would be lost in America." *Wise lady*, I thought.

One day on my way to the clinic I saw some Mexican soldiers in town. The captain approached me. "What exactly are you doing in this place?" He had a list of questions for me.

He turned out to be a very nice man. "May I see your camera?" He wanted me to give him my Instamatic camera so he could take pictures of the area and finish off my roll of film. "I am going to develop this film." I didn't really understand why this was necessary.

I had kept my camera with me at all times, as the villagers loved it when I took pictures of them. I was always looking for great shots to capture my experience in Chilar.

I figured I didn't have a choice, so I handed the captain my camera and the other exposed rolls. "You had better keep your word and send these back to me." I smiled at him and he nodded. For some reason I trusted that he would do as I asked.

I came to find out the soldiers were in the area looking for drugs. Unbeknownst to me, Sinaloa was a hotbed for drug trafficking. I had never encountered any drugs, including marijuana. The soldiers stayed a few days and left when they were satisfied that there were no drugs growing in the fields.

True to his word, two weeks later, the captain sent my camera and pictures to me along with a nice note. Having the photographs in hand was a real treat, because I could share them with the villagers who were delighted to see themselves. To them, it was magic that a little box could produce such images of them.

Another "magic fact" that some of the villagers, including Jeronima, couldn't believe, was that American astronauts had walked on the moon five years before. One night when the moon was full, I told them this. I remember them laughing at me in disbelief. I don't think they ever did believe me.

Chapter 32

Adios, Chilar

My Farewell Procession

My final days in Chilar were very busy. Not only was I occupied with *consultas* at the clinic, but I also took time to visit with my favorite people. I was invited to eat with many families and spent as much time as possible with Jeronima.

    I pulled a few more teeth. One molar in particular was really tough and took a lot of force to pull out. Another tooth I pulled broke into bits and pieces because it was so rotten.

    Then I had a child come in from the town of Caballo Abajo with what looked like rheumatic fever. Following David's book, I treated him with antibiotics.

Nancy sent me a telegram telling me that the nursing schools in San Diego, Chico, and UC San Francisco had not accepted me. According to UCSF I was rejected for having too much experience.

Though I was disappointed, I realized this was a blessing in disguise. I would set my sights on applying to PA schools when I returned. These rejections opened up an exciting new door for me. I would not become a nurse after all. I would become a Physician Assistant.

How funny life is. What seems like a terrible disappointment oftentimes turns into the biggest blessing. This has pretty much been the story of my life; disappointments have always led me to new and exciting opportunities.

Although my last weeks were busy, they were also sad. It was sad for me, it was sad for Jeronima, and it was sad for the villagers. I couldn't believe six months had passed already. When I first came to Chilar, I thought six months would last forever. And now here we were, after so many horrific and wonderful and maturing experiences.

Ever since I had refused Crecencio's offer of marriage, I saw very little of him. He was busy working in his *milpa* on the side of the mountain, and sometimes he just slept there. I missed him and wondered if I had made a mistake by refusing his offer. Ultimately, I knew I had made the right decision.

The night before I left, I had a chance to visit with Crecencio. We talked for a long time and hugged, parting as friends. I thought this would be the last time I would ever see him, but as I mentioned earlier, I saw him again in the United States three years later when he came up in hopes of finding me and starting a new relationship.

April 14, 1975 had arrived. It would be my last day in Chilar. I placed all of my belongings on a burro. I would ride out on the back of the mule. All morning long, Jeronima and I were crying and hugging. We walked arm in arm down the street and slowly the rest of Chilar joined us in a parade of sorts.

Pancho would be my guide. He waited at the edge of town with the mules while the entire village walked with me. What a wonderful sendoff! The love I felt was incredible from everyone. Some were crying but all were somber.

The only face missing in the crowd was my Crecencio, but I understood why.

For the past six months, the villagers of Chilar had been my greatest teachers. They taught me what was really important in life and how to enjoy the little things, lessons that I've used all my life.

As we were nearing the edge of town, someone shouted, "Katalina, you can't go."

Then he asked, "Who is going to take care of us now?"

That one question stuck with me all my life. I realized that unlike the mentoring program used in Ajoya, I hadn't taught anyone to take my place. Although I was able to help them, I never taught them how to help themselves.

This was another important lesson I learned which affected my future. Because of this, I decided to not only be a provider in the PA profession, but to be a teacher as well. I wanted to make sure that every person I taught would provide the best care they could. I also felt it was very important to teach my patients how to care for themselves. I always made sure they understood their medical issues and what treatments were available.

I hugged everyone, and last of all Jeronima.

"Jeronima," I whispered under my breath, "I promise I will be back someday."

How strange it was to be leaving for good. I had grown to love Chilar and its inhabitants. I got on my mule, waved, thanked everyone and slowly turned to make my last trip to Ajoya.

So ended one of the most influential experiences in my life. Chilar, you changed me forever. My trip to Chilar truly was, for me, the journey of a lifetime.

> [As it turned out, I made four trips back to Chilar
> in the next few years,
> before my life got swallowed up
> by my job, my profession, and raising a family.]

xoxox

Afterword

Chilar: Journey of a Lifetime is filled with profound insights about human nature and human relationships that should inspire anyone seeking fullness of life. Kaye's courage, humility, humor, and loving spirit are on every page. She was meant to write this book.

It has been a true joy to assist Kaye in writing her story. Even as her health was failing, we had wonderful conversations as she mined memories of her time at Davis and her trip to Mexico. Though we were college roommates for just a short time, and lost touch completely for over twenty-five years, we reconnected as if no time had passed. Thank you, Facebook.

My visit to her home in April 2016 was a special time. Tom and Kaye made me feel so welcome, even through exhaustion and increasing discomfort.

Thank-you, Kaye. You lived your life with so much grace and so much love. You inspire us all.

Sherree Funk
July 2016

www.ingramcontent.com/pod-product-compliance
Lightning Source LLC
Chambersburg PA
CBHW030443300426
44112CB00009B/1147